HISTORY AND VIOLENCE IN ANGLO-IRISH LITERATURE

COSTERUS

NEW SERIES

VOL 71

Edited by

C.C. Barfoot, Hans Bertens and Theo D'haen

AMSTERDAM 1988

HISTORY AND VIOLENCE IN ANGLO-IRISH LITERATURE

Edited by

JORIS DUYTSCHAEVER

and

GEERT LERNOUT

ISBN : 90-5183-066-1 (C.I.P.)

TABLE OF CONTENTS

PREFACE

This volume presents a collection of papers read at the first Easter Conference on Anglo-Irish Literature at the University of Antwerp on April 9, 1986. All papers have been expanded and updated for publication, with the exception of Brendan Kennelly's keynote speech which has been printed with very few editorial revisions so as to keep its original flavour as a performance. The last contribution was not delivered at the conference, but its inclusion is justified by the fact that W.J.McCormack was associated with the University of Antwerp in the Fall term of 1987.

The name "Easter Conference" was chosen only for the pedestrian reason that it was scheduled during the Easter vacation, but also with a view to commemorating the seventieth anniversary of the Easter Rising, while refraining from giving the conference the character of a political celebration. The task set was rather to clarify working assumptions and complex issues in dealing with the relationship of history, violence and literature.

Grateful acknowledgement is made to the following publishers and persons for their gracious permission to quote from books published or written by them: to Oxford University Press for quotations from Derek Mahon's poems ("Courtyards in Delft" from *The Hunt by Night* and lines from "A Disused Shed in Co. Wexford" from *Poems 1962-1978*); to Faber and Faber for quotations from *The Collected Poems of Louis MacNeice* and from Brian Friel's *The Communication Cord* and *Selected Plays*; to the Dolmen Press for quotations from *Poems, 1956-1973* and *The Táin*; to Michael Longley for the quotation of "Wounds" and to James Simmons for the quotation of "Claudy"; to Secker and Warburg for the quotations from *The Newton Letter*, *Birchwood* and *Kepler*.

Joris Duytschaever
Geert Lernout

POETRY AND VIOLENCE

I would like to begin this talk by reading a poem to you - a translation into English of a poem originally written in Irish. It is called *Caoineadh Airt Uí Laoghaire - A Cry for Art O'Leary*. The poem was written by a woman, Eileen O'Connell. It is a cry of grief, of revenge, of love, of hatred, and of a deep, frustrated passion for justice. Art O'Leary was Eileen O'Connell's husband. He was shot by a man named Morris because he refused to sell his horse to Morris for five pounds. According to the 18th century penal law in Ireland, a Catholic had to sell his horse to a protestant, if the protestant asked him, for five pounds or under. O'Leary refused to sell his horse. Morris shot him. Eileen O'Connell composed her *Caoineadh* - her *cry* for her man. I chose this poem because it is a poem about various forms of violence - sexual, religious, political, forms of violence that occur again and again throughout Irish writing. But it is far more than that: here, the woman's passion is fiercely real; this fierce, passionate, violent reality creates the poem's momentum, its primal, driving, driven rhythms. It is, above all, a *cry* - a violent cry, *beyond* words, put *into* words. It intrigues me most of all for the way the woman's violent feelings are somehow changed even as they are expressed in this unrelenting rhythmical momentum.

In order to give an idea of this transfiguring rhythm, I shall read a few lines from the Irish, and then, *without comment*, pass straight into the English. Remember that the poem is a *cry* - the heart's pure violence, dragged down into language, elevated *by* it, and transfigured *in* it.

A Cry For Art O'Leary
(from THE IRISH OF EIBHLIN DUBH NI CHONAILL,
translated by Brendan Kennelly)

My love
The first time I saw you
From the top of the market
My eyes covered you
My heart went out to you
I left my friends for you

Threw away my home for you

What else could I do?

You got the best rooms for me
All in order for me
Ovens burning for me
Fresh trout caught for me
Choice meat for me

In the best of beds I stretched
Till milling-time hummed for me

You made the whole world
Pleasing to me

White rider of love!

I love your silver-hilted sword
How your beaver hat became you
With its band of gold
Your friendly homespun suit
Revealed your body
Your pin of glinting silver
Glittered in your shirt

On your horse in style
You were sensitive pale-faced
Having journeyed overseas
The English respected you
Bowing to the ground
Not because they loved you
But true to their hearts' hate

They're the ones who killed you
Darling of my heart

My lover
My love's creature
Pride of Immokelly
To me you were not dead
Till your great mare came to me
Her bridle dragging ground
Her head with your startling blood
Your blood upon the saddle
You rode in your prime

I didn't wait to clean it
I leaped across my bed
I leaped then to the gate
I leaped upon your mare
I clapped my hands in frenzy
I followed every sign
With all the skill I knew
Until I found you lying
Dead near a furze bush
Without pope or bishop
Or cleric or priest
To say a prayer for you

Only a crooked wasted hag
Throwing her cloak across you

I could do nothing then
In the sight of God
But go on my knees
And kiss your face
And drink your free blood

My man!
Going out the gate
You turned back again
Kissed the two children
Threw a kiss at me
Saying "Eileen, woman, try
To get this house in order,
Do your best for us
I must be going now
I'll not be home again."
I thought that you were joking
You my laughing man

My man!
My Art O'Leary
Up on your horse now
Ride out to Macroom
And then to Inchigeela
Take a bottle of wine
Like your people before you
Rise up
My Art O'Leary
Of the sword of love

Put on your clothes
Your black beaver
Your black gloves
Take down your whip
Your mare is waiting
Go east by the thin road
Every bush will salute you
Every stream will speak to you
Men and women acknowledge you

They know a great man
When they set eyes on him

God's curse on you, Morris
God's curse on your treachery
You swept my man from me
The man of my children
Two children play in the house
A third lives in me

He won't come alive from me

My heart's wound
Why was I not with you
When you were shot
That I might take the bullet
In my own body?
Then you'd have gone free
Rider of the grey eye
And followed them
Who'd murdered me

My man!
I look at you now
All I know of a hero
True man with true heart
Stuck in a coffin
You fished the clean streams
Drank nightlong in halls
Among frank-breasted women

I miss you

My man!
I am crying for you
In far Derrynane

In yellow-appled Carren
Where many a horseman
And vigilant woman
Would be quick to join
In crying for you
Art O'Leary
My laughing man

O crying women
Long live your crying
Till Art O'Leary
Goes back to school
On a fateful day
Not for books and music

But for stones and clay

My man!
The corn is stacked
The cows are milking
My heart is a lump of grief
I will never be healed
Till Art O'Leary
Comes back to me

I am a locked trunk
The key is lost
I must wait till rust
Devours the screw

O my best friend
Art O'Leary
Son of Conor
Son of Cadach
Son of Lewis
East from wooded glens
West from girlish hills
Yellow nuts budge from branches
Apples laugh like small suns
As once they laughed
Throughout my girlhood
It is no cause for wonder
If bonfires lit O'Leary country
Close to Ballingeary
Or holy Gougane Barra
After the clean-gripping rider

The robust hunter
Panting towards the kill

Your own hounds lagged behind you
O horseman of the summoning eyes
What happened you last night?
My only whole belief
Was that you could not die
For I was your protection

My heart! My grief!

My man! My darling!

In Cork
I had this vision
Lying in my bed:
A glen of withered trees
A home heart-broken
Strangled hunting-hounds
Choked birds
And you
Dying on a hillside
Art O'Leary
My one man
Your blood running crazily
Over earth and stone

Jesus Christ knows well
I'll wear no cap
No mourning dress
No solemn shoes
No bridle on my horse
No grief-signs in my house
But test instead
The wisdom of the law

I'll cross the sea
To speak to the King
If he ignores me
I'll come back home
To find the man
Who murdered my man
Morris, because of you
My man is dead

Is there a man in Ireland
To put a bullet through your head?

Women, white women of the mill
I give my love to you
For the poetry you made
For Art O'Leary
Rider of the brown mare
Deep women-rhytms of blood
The fiercest and the sweetest
Since time began
Singing of this cry I woman make
For my man

When one reads a poem like that, I think one is entitled to ask: what do we *do* with the violence of our emotions? And further - how is it that, so frequently, we, as critics, tend to obscure or hide or minimize the violence that is at the heart of such good poetry? Why do we *kill* poetry with intellectual politeness - with fatuous phrases like "It seems to me", when we should be saying "I believe". But even politeness has an ironic violence. You notice that I wrote (unconsiously) that politeness "kills". The poet who, in our times, has the reputation of dealing most frontally with violence is the English poet, Ted Hughes. When asked about violence in his poetry, he has this to say:

When my Aunt calls my verse "horrible and violent" I know what she means. Because I know what style of life and outlook she is defending. And I know that she is representative of huge numbers of people in England.
What she has is an idea of what poetry ought to be ... a very vague idea, since it's based on an almost total ignorance of what poetry has been written. She has an instinct for a kind of poetry that will confirm the values of her way of life. She finds it in the milder parts of Wordsworth if she needs supporting evidence. In a sense, critics who find my poetry violent are in her world, and they are safeguarding her way of life. So to define their use of the word violence any further, you have to work out just why her way of life should find the behaviour of a hawk "horrible" or any reference to violent death "disgusting", just as she finds any reference to extreme vehemence of life "frightening somewhow". It's a futile quarrel really. It's the same one that Shakespeare found the fable for in his *Venus and Adonis*, Shakespeare spent his life trying to prove that Adonis was right, the rational sceptic, the man of puritan good order. It put him through the

tragedies before he decided that the quarrel could not be kept up honestly. Since then the difficult task of any poet in English has been to locate the force which Shakespeare called Venus in his first poems and Sycorax in his last.
Poetry only records these movements in the general life... it doesn't instigate them. The presence of the great goddess of the primaeval world, which Catholic countries have managed to retain in the figure of Mary, is precisely what England seems to have lacked, since the Civil War... where negotiations were finally broken off. Is Mary violent? Yet Venus in Shakespeare's poem if one reads between the lines eventually murdered Adonis... she murdered him because he rejected her. He was so desensitized, stupefied and brutalized by his rational scepticism, he didn't know what to make of her. He thought she was an ethical peril. He was a sort of modern critic in the larval phase... a modern English critic. A typical modern Englishman. What he calls violence is a very particular thing. In ordinary criticism it seems to be confused a lot with anoter type of violence which is the ordinary violence of our psychotic democracy... our materialist, non-organic democracy which is trying to stand up with a bookish theory instead of a skeleton. Every society has its dream that has to be dreamed, and if we go by what appears on TV the perpetual tortures and executions there, and the spectacle of the whole population, not just a few neurotic intellectuals but the whole mass of the people, slumped every night in front of their sets... in attitudes of total disengagement, a sort af anaesthetized unconcern watching their dream reeled off in front of them, if that's the dream of our society, then we haven't created a society but a hell. The stuff of pulp fiction supports the idea. We are dreaming a perpetual massacre.[1]

In this assiduously-created hell, masquerading as a society, modern England may well be dreaming "a perpetual massacre", as it sits content and stupefied before the T.V. in a trance of symbiotic terror. The same is true of a good deal of modern Irish Life; Ireland is, in certain respects, as mummified by television violence and soap-operas as England or any other country. But in Ireland the massacre is not merely dreamed on television; it is *enacted* in the streets of Derry and Belfast and other places. The horrors of history are alive and well; and they have always been investigated, brooded on, and dramatised by Irish poets. Ireland is a small, relatively poor country - a small, congested place with a lot of hatred in it. There is a tourists' Ireland; there is a terrorists' Ireland; there is an Ireland of sentimentality, nostalgia, four green fields, Cathleen ni Houilhan, patriotic ballads sung

---

[1] "Ted Hughes and Crow", *London Magazine*, January 1971, p. 5-7.

in pubs to the musical accompaniment of Guinness being gulped; an Ireland of image-making, flawless middle-class Catholic respectability, flawless Protestant politeness with nice accents and good taste; an Ireland of endless opinions, comments, judgements, talk (always talk), and letters to the *Irish Times* about the first cuckoo of the year, and the last true Republicans of the century.

And there is an Ireland, increasingly, of money, with all the polished, ruthless violence that money can bring; an Ireland, increasingly, of big business and cut-throat competition; an Ireland that is busy burying peasant superstition and practising a new bourgeois style, with all that *that* means and implies. And meanwhile there are bombs in shops, in streets, outside police barracks; there are assassinations and revenge-killings and corrective kneecappings. And there are always the innocent victims of this savage, tireless historical process, this appetite for death. The kind of violence I'm talking about now, the violence engendered by history, is the violence of hatred. Hatred is a dynamic force, a stimulating, animating power. Hatred hates indifference. Hatred loves its own annihilating expression, wiping out distinctions between innocent and guilty, adult and child, man and woman. Hatred tolerates no humane hierarchies of kindness, gentleness, affection, considerateness. Hatred sneers at the futility of intellectual subtlety. And hatred is, above all, a devoted servant to a cause. Hatred revels in devotion, in an *act* of unswerving service to a cause. In serving that cause, whatever it be, hatred is *exemplary* in its attention to its own unshakeable purpose. Yeats captured the situation when he wrote:

> Out of Ireland have we come;
> Great hatred, little room
> Maimed us at the start;
> I carry from my mother's womb
> A fanatic heart;

The beat of that fanatic heart can be heard clearly and frequently in Irish poetry. Here is a typical poem about hatred at work. It is by James Simmons. It is a ballad called *Claudy*. Terrorists leave a car containing bombs, in a village. They go to a nearby town to telephone a warning. The phone doesn't work. The consequences are horrific. Good poetry captures *consequences*.

CLAUDY
A Ballad

The Sperrins surround it, the Faughan flows by,
at each end of Main Street, the hills and sky,

the small town of Claudy at ease in the sun
last July in the morning, a new day begun.

How peaceful and pretty if the moment could stop.
McIlhenny is straightening things in his shop,
and his wife is outside serving petrol, and then,
a child takes a cloth to a big window-pane.

McCloskey is taking the weight off his feet,
and McClelland and Millar are sweeping the street,
and, delivering milk at the Beaufort Hotel,
young Temple's enjoying his first job quite well.

And Mrs McLaughlin is scrubbing her floor,
and Artie Hone's crossing the street to a door,
and Mrs Brown, looking around for her cat,
goes off up an entry - What's strange about that?

Not much - but before she comes back to the road
that strange car parked outside her door will explode,
and all of the people I've mentioned, outside,
will be waiting to die, or already have died.

An explosion too loud for your eardrums to bear,
and young children squealing like pigs in the square,
and all faces chalk white and streaked with bright red,
and the glass and the dust and the terrible dead...

for an old lady's legs are ripped off, and the head
of a man's hanging open and still he's not dead.
He is screaming for mercy while his son stands and stares
and stares, and then, suddenly, quick, disappears.

and Christ! little Katharine Aikin is dead
and Mrs McCloskey is pierced through the head.
Meanwhile to Dungiven the killers have gone
and they're finding it hard to get through on the phone.

Lying under the increasingly bland surfaces of Irish life, are various degrees of pathological hatred.

At this point, I would like to say that I believe that poetry is the language of the heart, shaped, directed, controlled, moulded and ordered by its colleague, the sympathetic, vigilant and discriminating intelligence. Poetry pays attention to feelings; and it finds its life in these feelings. By paying attention, constant attention, poetry discriminates, defines, and celebrates what it discovers. Poetry, like hatred, is therefore a kind of education, demanding dedication. But where poetry is the language of the heart in all its human vacillation and uncertainty, hatred is the language (word-language or bomb-language or gun-language) - the language of the heartless in all its stamina and unfeeling devotion. A person in love is potentially happy, or, potentially, a victim; a person in hate is unquestionably beyond such possibility of fulfilment or vulnerability. A person in hate becomes the instrument of his hatred. His heart is a stone. And yet it could be argued that political and historical changes have been brought about by the stony-hearted. So any poem about this *kind* of violence must confront this problem, this contradiction: change, the sort of change that brings about new civilizations with, perhaps, accompanying great works of art, admired by the sensitive, analysed by structuralists and deconstructionists in a formal, sophisticated idiom - that sort of change is often brought about by men and women who have precious little time for the sweet fruits of civilization, the consolations of poetry, the challenges and comforts of art. At the roots of good taste lies barbarism. In museums reposes evidence of murder and massacres; enthroned kings and popes rule and advise, pronounce and pontificate, to a background of blood. Yeats put it cogently:

> Some violent bitter man, some powerful man
> Called architect and artist in, that they,
> Bitter and violent ment, might rear in stone,
> The *sweetness* that all longed for night and day,
> The *gentleness* none there had ever known -

Violence is the *begetter* of sweetness and gentleness. Murderous *disorder* is often the source of that beautiful, unruffled self-possession and order which are associated with style.

Men with fanatical political causes embody this contradiction; they, the agents of change, are driven by a purpose that cannot change.
The most interesting parts of Yeats's poem *Easter 1916* debate this problem of change and unchangingness. Yeats cannot solve it. His moral intelligence as a person is repelled by what his imagination senses to be brutally true. The law of nature, or the law of God, is the law of change. In Dublin, Yeats knew men whose lives were devoted to radical change. He saw these people as "Hearts with one purpose alone". All around them, everything changes in nature,

> Hearts with one purpose alone
> Through summer and winter seem

Enchanted to a stone
To trouble the living stream.
The horse that comes from the road,
The rider, the birds that range
From cloud to tumbling cloud,
Minute by minute they change;
A shadow of cloud on the stream
Changes minute by minute;
A horse-hoof slides on the brim,
And a horse plashes within it;
The long-legged moor-hens dive,
And hens to moor-cocks call;
Minute by minute they live:
The stone's in the midst of all.

Creatures that live from "minute to minute" consciously or unconsciously partake of the universal changes that never cease, either within or outside them. But if the heart's a stone, what price change? Yeats says of the revolutionaries that they may have been bewildered by "excess of love". He does not, in this poem, speak of hatred - and this is, I think, one of the poem's shortcomings. This evasiveness in the poem helps to account for its flag-waving, rhetorical conclusion. He *does* begin to explore the situation created by the fact that

Too long a sacrifice
Can make a stone of the heart.
O when may it suffice?

but the poem swerves away from that question and from further exploration with

- Enough
To know they dreamed and are dead.

Well, yes, they dreamed. And they acted too. And they set in motion these changes that have helped to produce a small, modern country. But did not that "excess of love" (if it *was* such, or such *only*) also lead to, or point the way towards, *both* the new middle-class Irish society, *and* the "Northern Troubles", as that warfare is called. The stony-heartedness that resists change within itself, *because* its sole purpose is change in society, becomes part of the forces that it helps to unleash. It has its own messianism. That messianism may, generations later, pick up willing disciples and devotees. In fact, such discipleship is inevitable, so that the unborn will be burdened, in their time, with the responsibilities of the "stony heart". Irish history is so riddled with violence, so packed with horrors and persecutions of various kinds, that any significant body of poetry *out* of Ireland *must* take account of both that violence and its consequences.

A young contemporary poet, Michael Longley, looks at history, and sees wounds, the wounds of people, the wounds of history. Longley is a Northern Unionist; his father fought for the English, with the Ulster Division, at the Somme. His father survived that war, and died later when his wounds turned to cancer. Longley links his father's death and burial with the burial of three young English soldiers, and the death of a bus-conductor, murdered by a youngster, a teenager, as the family prepared to watch television, after supper. I choose this poem, *Wounds*, because it depicts the consequences in a atmosphere of domestic normality. A boy, become the instrument of history's blind hatred, *kills*, because he himself is both victim and instrument. This poem is a striking example of the grotesque normality of that violence which is the consequence of previous violence which is itself the consequence of previous violence - and so on. What is appalling is the reader's realization of something about the very nature of violence - that is, its fertility, its spawning, helpless fertility, endlessly begetting itself in infinite form, like a demented Proteus.

WOUNDS

Here are two pictures from my father's head-
I have kept them like secrets until now:
First, the Ulster Division at the Somme
Going over the top with "Fuck the Pope!"
"No Surrender!": a boy about to die,
Screaming "Give 'em one for the Shankill!"
"Wilder than Gurkhas" were my father's words
Of admiration and bewilderment.
Next comes the London-Scottish padre
Resettling kilts with his swagger-stick,
With a stylish backhand and a prayer.
Over a landscape of dead buttocks
My father followed him for fifty years.
At last, a belated casualty,
He said - lead traces flaring till they hurt -
"I am dying for King and Country, slowly."
I touched his hand, his thin head I touched.

Now, with military honours of a kind,
With his badges, his medals like rainbows,
His spinning compass, I bury beside him

Three teenage soldiers, bellies full of
Bullets and Irish beer, their flies undone.
A packet of Woodbines I throw in,
A lucifer, the Sacred Heart of Jesus
Paralysed as heavy guns put out
The night-light in a nursery for ever;
Also a bus-conductor's uniform -
He collapsed beside his carpet-slippers
Without a murmur, shot through the head
By a shivering boy who wandered in
Before they could turn the television down
Or tidy away the supper dishes.
To the children, to a bewilderd wife,
I think "Sorry Missus" was what he said.

What is "civilised" in us must condemn violence, as leaders of governments do with predictable clichés and platitudes. These do not diminish the sincerity of leaders; but they *do* emphasise the ready-to-hand slogan-like quality of their condemnations, as if leaders sensed something hollow in their own rhetoric of condemnation. If what is "civilised" in us must condemn, what is exploratory and creative in us must enquire and ponder.

What *is* violence?

As I write this lecture, the ink from my pen is violating the whiteness of the paper. When I eat, I know (usually) that a creature had to be killed so that my stomach may be satisfied. Beautiful, and unbeautiful women are often wrapped in the skins of several animals. Men, women and children *walk*, their feet cosily wrapped in death. If, as a teacher, one plants an idea in a student's mind that may be partly responsible for, say, a gesture or act or word from that person which may cause hurt to another, is one violating that person? How much violence is there in education? How many victims of intellectual rape are there in Universities? How much "happy" home-life depends on silent, and silently, mutually agreed-on, forms of violence? How violent are so-called passive women? What violence lies in Daddy's concern, his future-moulding concern for his son? How much are children violated by parents, parents by children? What violence begins to be born in us when we are too embarrassed or bland or indifferent to confront the problem of violence in ourselves? And can the "struggle for control" lead to *other* forms of violence? Above all, perhaps, what violence is there in our *desire* to possess - to possess houses, cars, jobs, each other? One thing is sure - the violence engendered in us as a result of discovery and admission is less damaging than the violence, frequently disguised as morality, engendered in us when we lie to ourselves. That is why the poetry of recognition and admission, no matter how clumsy or awkward, must always be preferable to the poetry of stylish evasion. There are many examples of both *kinds* of poem in the work of the same poet . Yeats, Ireland's greatest poet, is a good example. When Yeats is *talking* about being noble or candid or dignified or distinguished or vaguely aristocratic or honest (God help us!) then I prefer to think that Yeats is - just talking. But, in the next poem or the next breath, Yeats can *admit* the violence in his nature, and, without mentioning a word about candour and honesty, he wins our hearts with his honesty and candour.

> You think it horrible that lust and rage
> Should dance attention upon my old age:
> They were not such a plague when I was young.
> What else have I to spur me into song?

There, in a nutshell, is the core of the matter. The imagination of a man or a woman can be *nourished* by the same violent feelings and forces which would most likely repel that same man or woman in his or her attempts to live an ordinary, decent life. The light of poetry often finds its origin in the darkness of our natures. It is no wonder at all that Plato banished poets from his ideal republic. Or so my classical friends tell me.

Because poetry is, among other things, an interrogatory art , an art of relentless questioning. Ibsen called poetry "the soul's tribunal": when we read poetry, *really* read it, we are putting ourselves on trial. Do some people relegate poetry to the level of mere entertainment, or consolatory escapism, precisely because the close, intense study of it can result in a brutal state of self-revelation? So we condemn what we are not prepared to confront.

Because Irish life has so many *kinds* of violence in it, Irish poets have responded in a great variety of ways. So far, I have, for the most part, concentrated on *public* manifestations of violence, and their consequences. Public institutions and the lives of private individuals meet in ways both obvious and subtle. In Ireland, the most powerful single institution is the Roman Catholic Church. Over 95% of the population are Catholic. The Church is omnipresent, omniscient, and, apparently, omnipotent in Ireland. It is a predominantly *male* institution, though there are nuns everywhere. Only recently have Irish women begun to show any defiance against the Church; women were content, or *seemed* content, to go along with the fact and the implications of male domination. No divorce! No contraception! Sexual pleasure, outside of marriage, is a sin! Even *within* marriage, the purpose of sex is the begetting of children. And this *must* be the purpose - even if the mother is ill. Serious illness is no excuse. Many Irish women have died because of this kind of tyrannical, male-clerical thinking.

The Irish poet who most confronted and demonstrated this kind of tyranny is Austin Clarke. His autobiography *Twice Round The Black Church* is a stirring account of his own experience in the Catholic Church, and of his life when he left it. In this passage, for example, he describes his first confession at the age of seven. What we witness is a clerical assault on a child's consciousness.

At seven I made my first confession. I cannot remember how and when I was prepared for the sacrament of penance. No doubt I conned the penny catechism in class and learned the sixth commandment, which forbids all looks, words and actions against the virtue of chastity, speech with bad companions, improper dances, immodest company keeping and indecent conversation. In eager anticipation I set forth, proud of having now attained to the theological age of reason and in awe, knowing that the confessor was the visible representative of Christ. I went up Mountjoy Street that morning on our side of the street, past the Protestant orphanage, Wellington Street corner, and glanced up at the big clock over the public house.

In Berkeley Road chapel, I read the name of Father O'Callaghan over a confessional and, kneeling down, waited till the last penitents had left. Then I opened the side door on the left of the confessional and found myself in the narrow dark recess and, in a minute, the panel was drawn back. I told my little tale of fibs, disobedience and loss of temper and then Father O'Callaghan bent towards the grille and asked me a strange question which puzzled me for I could not understand it. He repeated the question and as I was still puzzled he proceeded to explain in detail and I was disturbed by a sense of evil. I denied everythin but he did not believe me and, as I glanced up at the grille, his great hooknose and fierce eyes filled me with fear. Suddenly the panel closed and I heard Father O'Callaghan coming out of the confession box. He opened the side door and told me to follow him to the vestry. I did so, bewildered by what was happening. He sat down, told me to kneel and once more repeated over and over his strange question, asking me if I had ever made myself weak. The examination seemed to take hours though it must have been only a few minutes. At last, in fear and desperation, I admitted to the unknown sin. I left the church, feeling that I had told a lie in my first confession and returned home in tears but, with the instinct of childhood, said nothing about it to my mother.

That little drama begins in a confession-box. One can feel there, in that poem, the *power* of the priest over the child. And that power breeds in the child a sense of evil. And so it was, and often still *is*, not only with priests and children, but with priests and women. I would like to read you a poem by Austin Clarke which presents a woman going to confession, to a Redemptorist priest, a missioner. She tells him it is ten months since the birth of her last child. The Redemptorist priest says this is a sin; and he cannot forgive her until she conceives again. She protests a little, but in vain. She goes home, her husband makes love to her that Saturday night, she conceives, she dies giving birth. It is a simple, frightening parable of the power of priests over women; of the violence done by an institution against a single, fragile, vulnerable woman. And this poem is also an excellent illustration of the kind of poem that Austin Clarke perfected - imagistic, anecdotal, making use of dialogue and brief, vivid, effective moments of characterization. The poem is , in effect, a little drama, a small play in a confession-box as a result of which the woman dies and the priest goes on his proud, powerful way, self-inflated with rhetoric and images of hell-fire. One gets in this poem a sense of the male conspiracy between priest and husband which has always been strong in Ireland. It is the *woman* who suffers as a result of the violence implicit in the "morality" of the institution of which she is a member, and in the doctrines of which she, presumably, believes. The violence done to her, her actual death, is brought about by the very fact of her belief. One wonders how many women have died because of their sincerity.

There is a reference in this poem to Adam and Eve's; it is a church in Dublin. The poem is entitled *The Redemptorist*. It is important to realize that the dialogue takes place in the extremely *quiet* privacy of the confessional.

THE REDEMPTORIST

"How many children have you?" asked
The big Redemptorist.
                    "Six, Father."
                                "The last,
When was it born?"
                        "Ten months ago."
"I cannot absolve your mortal sin
Until you conceive again. Go home,

Obey your husband."
                    She whimpered:
                                        "But
The doctor warned me ..."
                    Shutter became
Her coffin lid. She twisted her thin hands
And left the box.
                    The missioner,
Red-bearded saint, had brought hell's flame
To frighten women on retreat:
Sent on his spiritual errand,
It rolled along the village street
Until Rathfarnham was housing smoke
That sooted the Jesuits in their Castle.
"No pregnancy. You'll die the next time,"
The Doctor had said.

                                        Her tiredness obeyed
That Saturday night: her husband's weight
Digging her grave. So, in nine months, she
Sank in great agony on a Monday.
Her children wept in the Orphanage,
Huddled together in the annexe,
While, proud of the Black Cross on his badge,
The Liguorian, at Adam and Eve's,
Ascended the pulpit, sulphuring his sleeves
And setting fire to the holy text.

What Austin Clarke gets at, in a ruthless, penetrating way, is the hypocrisy engendered by the violence of the institution of the Church, directed against its members, especially women. Some three thousand Irish girls go to England every year to have abortions there. This suits perfectly. There are, you see, no abortions in Ireland. That means we're pure. But you can have an abortion in England. Aren't the English terrible? As a race, we Irish are so casually hypocritical in such matters that it is almost unbelievable.

And yet, precisely because of this blend of tyranny, hypocrisy and oppression, Irish poets have always celebrated the integrity, energy and heroic common-sense of women. The best of O'Casey's plays are a celebration of women's courage and endurance. Joyce's *Ulysses* finishes with Molly Bloom's torrential affirmation of life. Later novelists such as John Mc Gahern, Brian Moore and Edna O'Brien concentrate much on women's fighting spirit. Beckett's understanding and presentation is profound and comprehensive. And Thomas Murphy's recent play, *Bailegangaire,* is a wonderfully poetic celebration of the sheer spirit and stamina of women.

Long before any of these writers, however, James Stephens wrote about the way some women fought against the bland tyranny of men (that sort of tyranny, of which even men *themselves* realize they are guilty.). I have chosen James Stephens because he is a rather neglected figure. He was a contemporary of Yeats: he was a tiny little man (he has been referred to as a leprechaun): he was an orphan who is said to have been helped, when very young, by various women who took pity on him. In his novels, *The Crock of Gold, Deirdre* and *The Demi-Gods*, in his short stories, especially *Hunger*, and in many of his poems, Stephens has his women fight against their oppressive circumstances. Above all, perhaps, he is interested in how certain women fight for their *identity* in a world where so many forces combine to undermine that identity. In exploring woman's identity, Stephens discovers the well-springs of his own compassion as a poet: he finds out the direction of his deepest sympathies. In *this* poem, *The Red-Haired Man's Wife,* Stephens reveals the violence inherent in man's sacred structures, such as marriage. These structures are created by man, and sanctioned by man's God. This poem always reminds me of a line from Webster's play, *The Duchess of Malfi.* It is spoken by the Duchess herself, after she has experienced violence, horror and humiliation. She says *I am Duchess of Malfi still.* Here's Stephen's poem, in which the woman realizes and protests against the bland tyranny she senses is at the heart of the marriage-union:

THE RED-HAIRED MAN'S WIFE

I have taken that vow!
And you were my friend
But yesterday - Now
All that's at an end;
And you are my husband, and claim me, and
   I must depend!

Yesterday I was free!
Now you, as I stand,
Walk over to me
And take hold of my hand;
You look at my lips! Your eyes are too
   bold, your smile is too bland!

My old name is lost;

My distinction of race!
Now, the line has been crossed,
Must I step to your pace?
Must I walk as you list, and obey, and smile
  up in your face?

All the white and the red
Of my cheeks you have won!

All the hair of my head!
And my feet, tho' they run,
Are yours, and you own me and end me,
  just as I begun!

Must I bow when you speak!
Be silent and hear;
Inclining my cheek
And incredulous ear
To your voice, and command, and behest;
  hold your lightest wish dear!

I am woman! But still
Am alive, and can feel
Every intimate thrill
That is woe or is weal:
I, aloof, and divided, apart, standing far,
  can I kneel?

Oh, if kneeling were right,
I should kneel nor be sad!
And abase in your sight
All the pride that I had!
I should come to you, hold to you, cling to
  you, call to you, glad!

If not, I shall know,
I shall surely find out!
And your world will throw
In disaster and rout!
I am woman, and glory, and beauty; I,
  mystery, terror and doubt!

I am separate still!
I am I and not you!
And my mind and my will,
As in secret they grew,

> Still are secret; unreached, and untouched,
>   and not subject to you.

That, from a woman's viewpoint, is a poem about violence within a certain kind of marriage. As a rule, Irish poetry (with a few recent exceptions) has not really begun to explore the actual violence contained in marriage. Almost a hundred years after Ibsen, Irish poets are still tentative in explorations of "married" violence. Around marriage there is an entire mythology of happiness, peace, hygiene, promise, renewal, generation, valid or legal or legitimate sexuality. The bride is in white, usually; the man is impeccable. This is the Big Day, the once-in-a-lifetime event (especially if you happen to be an Irish Catholic). The implication of the Big Day is that marriage will lead to various forms of fulfilment. And no doubt it does, in certain cases. But in many other cases, it leads to other states, other conditions. It locks two people together in what can be a kind of violent, exclusive intimacy, a private arena where each can throw the other to the emotional lions. The *togetherness* of mariage *can* be based on a recognition of the silent violence of the atmosphere in which the couple live, discover each other, look at each other, renew each other. In this respect, violence is a kind of education, a private enlightenment, a schooling in forms of determination and continuity. Here is Thomas Kinsella's poem, *Remembering Old Wars:*

REMEMBERING OLD WARS

What clamped us together? When each night fell we lay down
In the smell of decay and slept, our bodies leaking,
Limp as the dead, breathing that smell all night.

Then light prodded us awake, and adversity
Flooded up from inside us as we laboured upright
Once moore to face the hells of circumstance.

And so on, without hope of change or peace.
Each dawn, like lovers recollecting their purpose,
We would renew each other with a savage smile.

At the back of most of the poems I've talked about is some kind of response to the violence inherent in sexuality. The Church uses this violence to keep women down; one man uses it to establish his own mastery, another to renew both himself and his mate while his mate does the same. It would appear that poetry tells us that violence is inevitable and universal, that it has to do with vital and consequential change, that it appeals to the imagination of a person even as it threatens or even appalls that same person's daily life. Or to put it another way: there are certain forces which, simultaneously, attract the imagination and repel the reason. Yeats's last poem *Under Ben Bulben* is a celebration of what violence can lead to.

> You that Mitchel's prayer have heard
> "Send war in our time, O Lord!"
> Know that when all words are said
> And a man is fighting mad,
> Something drops from eyes long blind,
> He completes his partial mind,
> For an instant stands at ease
> Laughs aloud, his heart at peace.
> Even the wisest man grows tense
> With some sort of violence
> Before he can accomplish fate,
> Know his work or choose his mate.

The imagination instinctively realizes that violence exists everywhere, and has its own purpose. It goes further: violence is a kind of motive-power, a sort of emotional fuel, a key to developed action, a source of creative thinking, a restless, stirring, challenging origin of art and civilization.

Poetry, like the moth to the flame, is drawn towards violence. But poetry does not perish because of this attraction. In fact, poetry is animated, vitalized, refreshed by the contact. This is so, I think, because poetry is neither moral nor immoral. It is amoral, it exists beyond conventional morality. If poetry merely reflected conventional morality, it would exist only in Christmas bards and after-dinner speeches. But poetry creates its own new fierce, vigorous code of morality. It was Synge who said that "before verse can be human again, it must learn to be brutal." This is the real crux. If poetry is to be real, challenging, primitive and sophisticated at once, then it must observe and imitate that fundamental principle of life: in a million different ways, under the guise of politeness, concern, do-gooding, converting, enlightening, educating, loving, - people do violence to each other. *Not* to perceive and explore this in poetry is to open the floodgates of sentimentally and sententious moralizing. That is why I personally believe that poetry, far from being consolatory and uplifting like some Victorian pill to send you asleep, radiant with beautiful thoughts, poetry is dangerous, particularly if it is constantly and attentively read. Not all of it is like this; but a surprising amount of it is.

Let us look, for example, at Yeats's *Leda and the Swan*. It is a poem about rape. The poem does not condemn rape; neither does it condone it; it *presents* it. And yet, if the poem could be said to teeter between condemning and condoning, I think that, after many readings, it could be argued that phrases such as "feathered glory", "loosening thighs", "strange heart", "white rush", and the sheer power of "engenders there" - all these veer towards a dramatization of the *energy* of the rapist, and not the plight of the victim. In the *present* act of violence, the future is born. Violence begets violence. Agamemnon is dead at the moment of the rape of Leda. Time and its fierce dramas are concentrated, focussed in that violent sexual act. We are appalled at the barbarism of the truth. The god, in the shape of a swan, rapes the girl. The poem, beautifully made, contains this violence within its elegant framework. The formal elegance makes the violence more savagely real, and forces the intellect to accommodate, in one mental feat, the co-incidence of act and consequence. Morality, as we tend to understand it, has no place here. The present is furiously incensed, that the future may be unleashed.

> A sudden blow: the great wings beating still
> Above the staggering girl, her thighs caressed
> By the dark webs, her nape caught in his bill,
> He holds her helpless breast upon his breast.
>
> How can those terrified vague fingers push
> The feathered glory from her loosening thighs?
> And how can body, laid in that white rush,
> But feel the strange heart beating where it lies?
>
> A shudder in the loins engenders there
> The broken wall, the burning roof and tower
> And Agamemnon dead.
>   Being so caught up,
> So mastered by the brute blood of the air,
> Did she put on his knowledge with his power
> Before the indifferent beak would let her drop?

Poetry tends to recognize and demonstrate what a conventional morality will tend to outlaw and condemn. The imagination, when it is probing, serves no system, obeys no law but its own longing for exciting truth. What we call "violence" is only a part of that excitement; gentleness, love, pity and mercy also come under its defining and dramatising scrutiny. Many of us tend to be like Ted Hughes's aunt - we tend to find a poetry that *confronts* violence somehow violent in itself, as if a poem were, *totally*, confined to its theme. It is not. A poem is limited only by the extent to which it fails to explore and present, as fully and truthfully as possible, the particular emotional world it has chosen, or been compelled by perhaps very instinctive forces, to explore and present. Ironically, Ted Hughes's aunt may well be a good, albeit reluctant, guide to the value of "violent" poetry. The more disgusted she is, the better the poem is likely to be. Most of us *do* find violence frightening and disgusting; but this doesn't mean, of course, that a poem succesfully presenting that same violence is disgusting and/or frightening. But, long before Victorian times, and certainly *after* Victorian times, there are many people who like to see poetry as "beautiful", "consolatory", "uplifting", "edifying", "beneficial to the soul". It may, indeed, be all these things: but it can also achieve the effect of the *opposite* of all these things: ugly, distressing, dangerous, even degrading, playing havoc with the spirit, if sensitively read. The treatment of violence in Irish poetry tells us that poetry cannot be denied its own full, adventurous, enquiring life. It will not be labelled, safely categorized, put into classified boxes.

Poetry, by definition, is always breaking through boundaries and categories. To try to inhibit or limit that function is to do violence to the very nature of poetry, to make it the sweet, biddable, musical slave of our expectations. The poetry that deals with violence is more concerned with its *own* compulsions than with the expectations of others. It will not flatter or comfort or console; it will disturb, challenge, even threaten. Above all, it threatens our complacency. And, in a world that seems hell-bent on its own destruction, that threat to complacent unawareness is a valuable service. We are brought into closer, more articulate contact with fiercely energetic forces which are at work both within and outside ourselves. The poems I have read and spoken about represent some of these forces; they demand that we look at what we call violence face to face. Reading becomes a kind of encounter with the repulsive, even the unspeakable. Returning from such encounters, we are more aware, more conscious. What we choose to do, or *not* to do, with our state of temporarily extended awareness, is our own affair. "Violent" poetry, the poetry of uncompromising consciousness, the poetry of hard, raw reality, continues to do its work of dramatic demonstration, of ruthless bringing-to-mind, of accusation and warning. This work, as I hope I have shown, is difficult, discomforting, and increasingly necessary.

Brendan Kennelly

TAIN AFTER TAIN
THE MYTHICAL PAST AND THE ANGLO-IRISH

> Gradualmente se vio (como nosotros)
> Aprisionado en esta red sonora
> De Antes, Después, Ayer, Mientras, Ahora,
> Derecha, Izquierda, Yo,Tú, Aquellos, Otros.
> *El Golem*

My aim here is to develop an imagological reading of the notion of a literary and cultural tradition; by which I mean that the synchronic preoccupations of imagological study -- i.e. the images that "nations" have of themselves and of foreigners at given points or periods in history -- may be usefully complemented by a diachronic approach, in which the concept of national identity is not defined by demographic appurtenances and current attributes or perceived characteristics, but as a set of inherited traditions and historical recognitions and appropriations.

Like all notions of national identity, the Irish one is ultimately something between an ideal and a stereotype. It exists in people's minds (both Irish people's and others') as an ideal to adopt or to reject, to pay allegiance to or to repudiate, to belong to or not. It is a point of reference from which one's individual position vis-à-vis the others can be gauged.

The notion of national identity is, then, an *image*. Such images are necessarily simplifications, models imposed on the contradictory multifariousness of actual reality. Hence we see that various, sometimes conflicting images of what constitutes "Irishness" can exist at different periods in history, or even simultaneously, side by side in the minds of Ulster Presbyterians, Gaelic Leaguers, German tourists and British comedians. In all these avatars, such an image can only exist by the grace of something rather like a willing suspension of disbelief, a tacit readiness to disregard whatever diverges from the image in actual reality, to register only the image's verifications, never its falsifications. If we have a certain idea of what "the Irish" are like, does that apply to all Irish, regardless of age, religion, social position, sex or regional background? And if we say that, of course, our idea applies to the "real Irish", to a "significant" or "characteristic" portion of the population, who then is to decide, and on what grounds, which Irish are more real, more significant, more characteristic than others? A nation's heterogeneity must needs be disregarded if a national image is to be convincing, i.e. free from self-contradictions. Reality can afford to be contradictory and incomprehensible; an image cannot. Rather than sharing in the anarchic freedom of reality, the *vrai*, it is bound by the stringent mimetic laws of realism, the *vraisemblable*.

All this is more or less received opinion in that branch of comparative literary studies known as imagology[1]: namely, that notions of national identity are ultimately received images, often rooted in the conventions and *imaginaire* of literature, consisting of a mythopoetic iconography applied to ideological purposes. One could add that an image of national identity is a result of selection and generalization: ingredients, traits and manners, are selected from the reservoir of available actuality, and then generalized as being somehow typical or characteristic. The result is a unification of diversity into a typified identity. I aim to show that a similar mechanism takes place on a diachronic axis.

A nation defines itself not only demographically, but also historically, in terms of its history, its heritage. That heritage does not, however, encompass the entirety of that nation's historical past; it is, rather, a selection from that past. Such a selection is further characterized by its timelessness, the fact that it has been liberated from the parameters of its chronological setting. The preterite of past reality becomes that of a fairy-tale's "Once upon a time" -- any time; the preterite is used ambiguously, for what is either a bygone reality or else a narrative. Such ambiguity can turn the Irish past into Irish history into "The Story of Ireland", where selected representatives of the Irish cause, like Brian Ború, Tone, O'Connell and Parnell are all *bien étonnés de se trouver ensemble* in an extra-temporal sanctuary. (Daniel-Henri Pageaux speaks of "le temps cyclique, reversible" of national images which are situated in "une sorte de temps mythique, en dehors de toutes limites précises: le 'in illo tempore' propre au mythe".[2]) This transcendence of the historical

---

[1] As regards the imagological approach, cf. the various publications by Hugo Dyserinck (a general *mise à point* being his article "Komparatistische Imagologie jenseits von 'Werkimmanenz' und 'Werktranszendenz'", *Synthesis* 9 (1982), 27-40) and of some of his students and collaborators in the Aachen Programme, e.g. M.S. Fischer ("Literarische Seinsweise und politische Funktion nationalbezogener Images. Ein Beitrag zur Theorie der komparatistischen Imagologie", *Neohelicon* 10 (1983), 251-74).

[2] D.-H. Pageaux, "Une perspective d'études en littérature comparée: L'imagerie culturelle", *Synthesis* 8 (1981), 169-85 (p. 176); elsewhere in the same article, Pageaux speaks of such stereotypes as "l'expression même d'un temps bloqué, le temps des essences" (p. 173). Another method of reading this anachronistical aspect in Irish national thought is developed by Oliver MacDonagh, who studies

barriers between the different periods of Irish history entails a fundamental principle of anachronism, justified by the invocation of Irish nationhood as a timeless, extra-historical entity. Much of the anachronisms we shall encounter in what follows here, can be explained from this fact.

As in the notion of a national heritage, so too in that of a literary tradition. Take, for example, English literature. What common ground, even linguistically, is there between Beowulf and Donald Barthelme, between Caedmon and Robert Coover? It may be answered that these names are linked at least by a historical continuum or continuity, by a "tradition", in the root sense of the term; and indeed such a tradition may exist -- But at least partly so as the result of a selection, of canonization, of a chronological accumulation of value judgements which acknowledge one forerunner while actively repudiating, or passively disregarding, another. In this sense, we can see that the notion of a tradition, like that of a national identity, is essentially an image, leading an affective existence in people's minds as a background against which the reading or writing act is historically situated and silhouetted. Such images of appurtenance to a national literary tradition can be seen to surface, for instance, in the works of T.H. White or J.C. Powys, or in John Gardner's retelling of the Beowulf saga under the title *Grendel*. Modern English or American authors will tend to look back to a tradition which is concurrent with the history of their language, English.

It is here that Anglo-Irish authors tend to take up a different position. Seamus Heaney and Thomas Kinsella write in English, and share that language with Barthelme, Pynchon, Gardner, Powys and White. But when they turn to their affective literary roots we see that these are not those of the language they write in, but instead lie in an utterly different language, Gaelic. Heaney and Kinsella do not turn to Beowulf and Malory but to the *Buile Suibhne*, to the *Lebor Gabála*, to the *Táin Bó Cuailnge*.

Which finally brings us to the Táin. The Táin, and the vicissitudes of its readings by a non-Gaelic audience are my test-case for some implications of the foregoing, and I would like to concentrate specifically on two Anglo-Irish versions: those of Lady Gregory and

---

the "Irish habit of historical thought" in his fascinating *States of Mind. A Study of Anglo-Irish Conflict 1780-1980* (London: George Allen & Unwin, 1983). Cf. also the interesting collection *The Invention of Tradition*, ed. Eric Hobsbawm and Terence Ranger (Cambridge: Cambridge University Press, 1983).

Thomas Kinsella.[3] I intend to assess these two versions, not as regards their literary merits or their fidelity to the original, but as instances of a selection and appropriation of a national literary heritage, instances of a more or less deliberate attempt to create a tradition, a link of continuity, between two different cultures, languages, and historical periods.

Let me begin by speaking a word in vindication of Lady Gregory. A patronizing tone is often heard when this woman's work is discussed; but in fact her version of the Táin Bó Cuailnge was the first time that the Ulster cycle as a whole was made accessible to the broader reading public. (I have chosen to disregard here the retellings by Standish O'Grady, which reflect the Táin no more faithfully than Tennyson's *Idylls of the King* reflect Malory.) Celtic philology had only just begun to decipher, edit and translate, in a scholarly and fragmentary fashion, the source texts; and until Lady Gregory collected these, did some translation of her own and brought out her rendering of these myths and sagas, the centre stage in the Gaelic *imaginaire* had been held by the stories and characters of the later cycle of Fionn mac Cumhaill and Oisín. There would be but very little exaggeration in the contention that we owe the entire Ulster cycle -- as literary rather than philological material -- to Lady Gregory; which makes her achievement equal in importance to that of Charlotte Brooke a hundred years previously. Furthermore, if we read *Cuchulain of Muirthemne* side by side with its original (as edited and translated by Cecile O'Rahilly), we cannot but be struck by the deftness, completeness, elegance and fidelity of Lady Gregory's translation. At the same time, however, such a comparison illustrates that a literary translation (like Lady Gregory's) and a scholarly one (like Cecile O'Rahilly's) are two quite different things. The former is far more deeply influenced by considerations of taste; and it is this matter of taste which I want to discuss here -- taste, that is, as one of those criteria by which a heritage, a tradition is selected from the multifarious and contradictory remains of the past. Yet let me say that if I discuss the various ways in which these literary versions (Kinsella's no less than Gregory's) diverge from the original, I do NOT do so by way of a stricture or imputation of infidelity; on the contrary, the aim is merely to illustrate that both approach their

---

3 The following texts have been used: Augusta Gregory, *Cuchulain of Muirthemne. The Story of the Men of the Red Branch of Ulster Arranged and Put into English by Lady Gregory. With a Preface by W.B. Yeats*. 5th ed. (Gerrards Cross: Colin Smythe, 1970). Thomas Kinsella, *The Táin, Translated from the Irish Epic Táin Bó Cuailnge by Thomas Kinsella, with Brush Drawings by Louis Le Brocquy*(London/Dublin: Oxford University Press/Dolmen; 1970). Cecile O'Rahilly (ed./trl.), *Táin Bó Cúalnge from the Book of Leinster* (Dublin: Dublin Institute for Advanced Studies, 1967). Referred to here as LG, TK and CO'R, respectively.

source-text, not with a scholar's disinterestedness or antiseptic self-effacement, but rather with a writer's creativity and desire of appropriation, re-creation.

Lady Gregory undertook her work (which eventually appeared in 1902) in an atmosphere of revivalism and cultural nationalism. Her contemporaries (Standish O'Grady, Douglas Hyde, young Yeats) asserted a cultural greatness for the Irish nationality to counterbalance Ireland's political subordination under Great Britain. They did so by glorifying Ireland's Gaelic past. A glorification of the Gaelic past was nothing new. It had started with Macpherson's Ossian and Walter Scott's romantic novels, and such Scottish activities had had important repercussions in Ireland; these had resulted in a well-defined iconography of what the Gaelic past must have been like: heroic, full of romantic appeal, with a touch of melancholia and mysticism, and a dash of Rousseauesque simplicity and artlessness.

Furthermore, Irish cultural nationalism was becoming distinctly populist in tendency. Around the same time, a battle raged within the ranks of Gaelic revivalists as to the linguistic standards which were to be applied to the nearly extinct, now to be resuscitated language: was one to emulate the literary language of the eighteenth century, as used in the last written records before the Gaels were pauperized into illiteracy? Or was one to use the more eroded and less standardized, more divergent language as spoken by the contemporary people in various dialects? In the event, the more populist wing carried the day, and the linguistic ideal was to be the spoken, living, popular language, *caint na ndaoine*.

Finally, it must be pointed out that the revival movement, for all its populism, was middle-class, urban and paternalistic. If it canonized the popular spoken language, it treated the speakers themselves with a distinctly patronizing attitude, purveyors to Dublin tourists of local colour and rustic quaintness. Peasants who could prove to Gaelic League inspectors that they habitually used the language were to be rewarded with boy-scout baubles such as diplomas or medals, and their actual poverty and hardship were idealized as picturesque simplicity and homeliness.

Attitudes like these were shared to no small extent by Lady Gregory -- though she was no tourist, but lived separated from the rural population by class barriers rather than by physical distance. To begin with, her version of the Táin is materially influenced by the contemporary Victorian iconography of the romantic Gaelic past. For instance, the very word "queen" must have had an altogether different meaning for Lady Gregory than for the ancient Gaels -- a meaning strongly influenced by connotations from the realm of poetic romance and romantic fairy-tale, as well as by a pre-Raphaelite or *fin-de-siècle* ideal of exalted womanhood (with a dash of the femme fatale, perhaps); that, anyway, is the impression we get of Deirdre, Maeve or Findabair, proud admirable superwomen whose beauty subdues heroes, who never stoop to fornicate or menstruate and who are perfect material, therefore, for the poets and playwrights of the Irish Literary Revival.

The genteel sexlessness of *Cuchulain of Muirthemne* and its respectable protagonists has been repeatedly pointed out, usually with a knowing twentieth-century snigger, as an example of the prudery imposed by the Victorian lady. Can it be considered a deliberate bowdlerization, however? I think that that would be an overstatement. The one instance where Lady Gregory admits as much, is when the original lets Cuchulain be confronted (and stared down) by the Ulster women "exposing all their nakedness and shame to him".[4] Lady Gregory lets them be merely topless, and goes as far as excusing what she herself considered an infidelity by stating that priests would have considered a more faithful translation indecent:

> It was to shock Cuchulain's modesty it was done, as we know by his hiding his face, & the partial undressing was enough for that. Priests might legitimately say the other called up an indecent picture.[5]

The prudery is presented as that of the Irish Catholic reading public, rather than of the Anglo-Irish Protestant translator. The suppression of other possible "indecencies" -- references to urine, excrement, menstruation and copulation -- may, I think, be considered as part of the more general de-barbarization of the Táin and of its wild stalwart heroines; and such a de-barbarization must have been necessarily attendant upon the very fact of the Táin's being read by late nineteenth-century eyes. It is an unobjectionable part of the translator's task to interpret and naturalize the obscurities in which superhuman acts of prowess or battle feats are described, as in the case of the hero Cuchulain. Much as Tennyson imposed a nineteenth-century ethos of "the perfect gentleman" on king Arthur, so too did Lady Gregory conceive of her Cuchulain as a Gaelic hero in the Oscar or Diarmaid mode; the grotesqueness of the original, whose sign of heroic beauty is the fact that he has seven fingers and toes on each hand and foot, and that he has three (or elsewhere, seven)

---

[4] CO'R p. 171; in the original ibid p. 32, 1. 1189, "do thócbáil a nnochta & a nnáre dó".

[5] Lady Gregory to Yeats as quoted by Gerard Murphy, in his preface to LG, pp. 8-9.

pupils in each eye, is expurgated. If, in the original, Cuchulain is said to strip the bark off trees in Asterix-like fashion, i.e. between his bare fingers and toes, such a hyperbolic detail is suppressed by Lady Gregory (p. 155); his odd and characteristic "warp-spasm", i.e. a convulsion which seizes him in moments of battle frenzy and which is described in grotesquely hyperbolical terms, is reduced by Lady Gregory to a mere "hero's halo" which prettily shines around his head. Such smaller instances, like the toning-down of Cuchulain's appearance and warp-spasm, are part of a similar attitude as that which will gloss over the passing references to pelvic matters. And at the same time it should be pointed out that Lady Gregory seems frank enough by Victorian standards: she is quite straightforward when it comes to Cuchulain's admiration for the swell of Emer's breasts, etc.

Another aspect of Lady Gregory's imposition of a contemporary outlook on the unfamiliarity of the Táin lies in the fact that she presents "the Gaels" as a unitary, if feud-ridden nation comprising all the inhabitants of Ireland. This is in accordance with the nationalist outlook of her time, which defended Ireland's radical un-Englishness with the idea that the "real" Ireland was Gaelic, overlaid by uncharacteristic Norman and English intrusions. In fact, however, the Táin testifies to a period in Irish history when there was no such thing as a homogeneously "Gaelic" Ireland, when the country was inhabited by a number of different tribes who were at war with each other. The *Ulaid* or men of Ulster are presented as a different nation or tribe from the *fir Hérend* or "men of Éire", much as the *Gailéoin* or Leinstermen are wary strangers within the Connacht army. These deep tribal divisions are not recognized as such by the nineteenth-century translator for whom "the Gaels" are the homogeneous ethnic unity of all non-English, non-Norman, "Irish Ireland".

Not only does Lady Gregory translate the Táin according to her own, Victorian idea of what the Gaelic past must have been like, she is also a product of her times in her curious combination of populism and paternalism. The populism appears at its most obvious in the fact that she translated the stark and archaizing Gaelic of the original, not into standard English but into her equivalent of *caint na ndaoine,* the popular spoken language: the dialect of Eastern Galway, Kiltartanese. In the mind of the revivalists of the period, "Gaelic" was automatically interchangeable with a notion of a popular, rural, oral culture; which may have been true enough in a contemporary frame of reference, but which was certainly at odds with the aristocratic warlordism which was the Gaelic culture as reflected in the Táin. The proud, cold brutality of the original is expressed in an idiom which is homely and slightly naive; the detached elegance of the chronicler's voice in the original becomes the voice of a storyteller by the fireside spinning a yarn of the days of yore. For Kiltartanese was the idiom which Lady Gregory learned from the storytellers whom she went visiting to collect oral materials; and indeed the translator's dedication "To the people of Kiltartan" makes it clear that Lady Gregory herself saw the Táin largely in an oral, storytelling frame of reference, and that to "revive" this material meant to link it back to the "living", oral tradition:

> My Dear Friends: -- When I began to gather these stories together, it is of you I was thinking, that you would like to have them and be reading them. For although you have not to go far to get stories of Finn and Goll and Oisin from any old person in the place, there is very little of the history of Cuchulain and his friends left in the memory of the people, but only that they were brave men and good fighters, and that Deirdre was beautiful. (p. 5)

Lady Gregory is in fact trying to make the Táin "go native", to render it more folksy. As a result she projects her own image of what the natives, her contemporaries, are like on the characters of her ancient source-text: a typical example of that anachronism which we have seen to lie at the very core of the notion of a tradition. Consequently, she decides, as she tells the people of Kiltartan, to leave out "a good deal I thought you would not care about for one reason or another": the originals' characters are conformed to contemporary pre-expectations. As in the case of the priests who would object to full frontal nudity, Lady Gregory's strictures are not presented as her own, but are a projection into her reading public. "My dedication shows clearly enough that I have done all from the peasant point of view".[6]

In this last attitude some of the paternalism of the Anglo-Irish bourgeoisie and gentry vis-à-vis the rural Irish already shines through. And if one takes a closer look at this paratextual packaging of the Táin, with racy dialect and dedication and all, and takes into account the tell-tale fact that Lady Gregory hides her own prudery behind the one she imputes to the priests of Ireland and the people of Kiltartan, it becomes obvious that those people of Kiltartan are in fact little more than a pretext. Is this book really intended for the use of the people of Kiltartan to whom it was dedicated? What would they make of Yeats's notes, where he speaks with characteristic pomposity of poetry being a "habit of mind caught as in the beryl stone of a Wizard?" (p. 266) Would they even have been able to read, or, if so,

---

[6] Lady Gregory to Yeats as quoted by Murphy, *ibid.*, p. 9.

to afford or to obtain a book published by John Murray, of Albemarle Street in London? And if the use of Kiltartanese is, in a sense, a shibboleth of true racy Irishness, is it the original text or the translator who stands in need of such legitimation? The people of Kiltartan are what they already had been to Lady Gregory before: mediators of Gaelic culture to a non-Gaelic audience. They are so even here, in providing to Lady Gregory a purported pseudo-audience and idiom through which she can claim legitimacy in her approach and appropriation of an old Irish saga. By invoking her Kiltartan connections, the modern Anglo-Irish lady can appropriate an ancient Gaelic text as if it were part of her own tradition.

Translation is, in this respect, an act of appropriation: works from one literary tradition are adopted, transmitted into a different one. The notion of translation presupposes, however, that in the process that work undergoes a change. It is not transmitted in its pristine state but in an adapted form; and often one can see that besides the linguistic change of clothes, other coatings are used in order to let this alien body be accommodated smoothly by its new, non-congenital milieu. In the case of Lady Gregory there was the buffer of Kiltartanese as the invocation of a common denominator between translator and source-text. Furthermore we can often see accretions of a paratextual nature around the text itself;[7] in the case of the Táin we see the unfamiliarity of the text mitigated by paratextual coatings, such as Lady Gregory's dedication to the people of Kiltartan, Yeats's Preface and note, and Lady Gregory's own notes which are of a bibliographical nature and which give the English pronunciation of Gaelic names (all for the benefit of the people of Kiltartan, no doubt).

It is relatively easy to recognize Lady Gregory's imagotypical projections into her original, since they were made from a bygone, Victorian ethos, recognizable in its unfamiliarity. It may be more difficult to register the points in which Thomas Kinsella projects his values into the Táin, since these values are modern ones and so common and foregrounded to us contemporaries that they may not be easily recognized. Yet I hope to show that there are inner tensions and contradictions in Kinsella's translation which are not unlike those in Lady Gregory's, and which are indicative of a similar mechanism of appropriation and projection.

---

[7] I use the word *paratext* in the sense as coined by Gérard Genette (Cf. his *Palimpsestes. La littérature au second degré*. Paris: Seuil, 1982, p. 9; and his *Seuils* (Paris: Seuil, 1987), as all typographical material which facilitates the presentation of a text to a reader without being in itself part of that text (page numbers, chapter headings, illustrations, title pages, blurbs, etc.)

One point which both translations have in common is the importance of paratextual coatings. Kinsella's Táin ends with textual footnotes and is preceded by a translator's note and acknowledgements, an artists's note, an introduction, three maps, a list of further reading on the subject, and a glossary of pronunciation of Irish words. After all that, it opens, not with the Táin itself, but with a section entitled "Before the Táin", which contain the *rémscéla* or preliminary/ancillary tales giving the background to some situations in the main body of the Táin itself. The Táin itself occupies only two thirds of the book entitled "The Táin". Finally, the presentation of the text is materially influenced by Louis Le Brocquy's brush drawings.

Those illustrations are, perhaps, a good way into a discussion of Kinsella's version of the Táin. As the artist says himself, they aim to be as "impersonal as possible", so as to do justice to the fact that the story they illustrate "owes its existence to the memory and concern of a people over some twelve hundred years" (p. viii). As a result they are deliberately shapeless, evocative rather than representational; they resemble, if anything, the blots of a Rorschach test. At the same time they are as impersonal as Rorschach tests and, despite the artist's intention, as deeply personal as such tests are.

The Táin itself, in all its textual and cultural obscurity, is such a Rorschach text; whatever we do with it, must in some way be illustrative of our own concerns. Even the very alienness and impersonality which are features which loom large over Thomas Kinsella's presentation of the text, must necessarily cease to be the Táin's own impersonality and alienness, and become expressive of Kinsella's own, latter-day poetics. Nowhere is this more obvious than in what is perhaps the most remarkable and interesting aspect of his translation, namely the passages of *rosc* and *retoiric*: runs of stepped lines worded extremely obscurely, the most archaic and incomprehensible enclosures of the Táin. Kinsella has here attempted a task which scholars have mostly shied away from: namely, to give an English rendering of these verbal ink-blots. These "translations" are no mean achievement and belong in any anthology of Kinsella's best poetry; but they are free projections of Kinsella the poet, inspired by dark hints in the original, rather than "translations" proper. In Kinsella's own words:

> The aim has been to produce passages of verse which more or less match the original for length, ambiguity, and obscurity, and which carry the phrases and motifs and occasional short runs that are decipherable in the Irish. (p. xii)

Yet, a dilemma lurks here, and we can follow its wake throughout Kinsella's version of the Táin: that he wishes to present us with an unrefined version of the Táin; but conscious unrefinement, or even the conscious maintaining of unrefinement, is a self-contradiction. It calls for the very thing it disavows: subtlety. Kinsella is highly subtle in being coarse or obscure. The brutality of the original becomes the cruelty of *A Technical Supplement*; the grotesqueness and irregularities of the primitive become those of modern primitivism, of the poet who keeps African masks in his study. The ink blot becomes a bird, a warrior.

The repercussions of this dilemma are at work throughout Kinsella's Táin. On the one hand, he constantly valorizes the coarse, primitive and grotesque elements of the more primitive version of the Táin; the oldest version of the Deirdre story, for instance, is considered superior to the later ones (p. vii), and although Kinsella is appreciative of Lady Gregory's translation, his main criticism is that she had "[refined] away the coarse elements and [rationalized] the monstrous and gigantesque" (p. vii) -- these being the elements which seem to appeal most to him. Yet Kinsella criticizes the very faithfulness of an earlier scholarly translation (by Winifred Faraday) on the grounds that it is "difficult to read with any pleasure, partly because it transmits the flaws of the text so accurately" (p. x), and opts himself for a good deal of that refinement and rationalization which he had reproached Lady Gregory with. "As far as possible," he says, "the story has been freed of inconsistencies and repetitions. Obscurities have been cleared up and missing parts supplied from other sources" (p. xi). Even so, the endnotes often contain remarks where Kinsella points out the inconsistencies of the original and disclaims, as it were, responsibility for such oddities. It is as if Kinsella is vacillating, undecided whether or not to interpose himself between the reader and the obscure original, whether or not to sacrifice the original's genuineness for his translation's readability; accordingly, his disclaimers of responsibility for inconsistencies or narrative flaws in the original typically employ a guardedly impersonal phraseology.[8]

One of the most characteristic features of Kinsella's treatment regards his use of proper names. These are all given in their old Irish

---

[8] For example: lists "are given", nomenclature "is discussed", a name-form "is used"; when the reader is to notice something, a suggestion is made to the effect that "It will be noted"; when the translator/annotator announces his decision not to point out further anomalies, he puts it that "It is not proposed to note all such inconsistencies". Cf. notes to pp. 2, 23, 25, as well as others. Kinsella consistently seems to dodge the use of the first person in his notes.

forms: Medb rather than Maeve, Derdriu rather than Deirdre. That may be a matter of consistency, and of faithfulness to the original orthography; but Kinsella takes this to the point where even geographical names are given in their Old Irish forms: the Shannon (modern Irish: Sionann) is named as Sinann, Teltown or Tailte is Tailtiu, and when the Connacht army camps in Cúil Sibrille, the name is glossed as "Cenannos, as it is now called" (p. 72). It is now called Kells, or in Irish Ceanannas; but certainly not Cenannos. At the same time the reader is made acutely aware that such names have a reference in real geography, for we are supplied with maps showing us the actual location of Cúil Sibrille and Tailtiu. There seems to be a conflict of intent here: on the one hand we are meant to recognize the geographical references in the Táin, on the other hand the names themselves are kept deliberately alien.

From which I would like to draw the following conclusion: Kinsella's version of the Táin is marked by a polarity of motivation, which is at the same time national and exoticist. An ancient culture is mediated to a modern readership and presented as an updating of the country's own cultural heritage. The names are those of a familiar, traditional *imaginaire* and culture-political iconography, the places are shown to lie in the very same country where centuries later this book is being published. That is the "national" aspect of Kinsella's Táin: it establishes a link between modern, English speaking Ireland and the Ireland of the ancient Gaelic-speaking warriors.[9] At the same time there is, however, an exoticizing element: for what obviously fascinates Kinsella most are the differences between the modern European ethos and the barbarism and heroism of the Táin, which can appeal to his own poetic sensibility, with its grotesque descriptions of battle frenzy, its cold, matter-of-fact brutality, its enigmatic feats of prowess, its casual, off-hand honesty in matters of sex and excretion. Here as in the nomenclature, Kinsella attempts to show how deeply different ancient Celtic culture was from our own christian/humanist tradition. That is the other pole, that of exoticism. The Anglo-Irish poet is in the extraordinary position that he can approach the cultural tradition of his native country from this tension between nationality and exoticism, that his "own" tradition (or what he claims, adopts, or subscribes to as such) is at the same time familiar and alien -- as it was for the language revivalists who rewarded native speakers with a colonialist liberality of beads and mirrors. It is this tension between national appurtenance and exoticist fascination which, I think, underlies the one between Kinsella's valorization of obscurity and

---

9 In his poem "The Route of the Táin" (in *New Poems 1973* (Dublin: Dolmen, 1973)), Kinsella speaks of aiming to "enrich the present / honouring the past" (p. 57).

archaism, and his act of rendering and translating, and thereby destroying, that selfsame obscurity and archaism.

Things are more complicated than that, however. It would be a simplification to speak of Lady Gregory's or Thomas Kinsella's relationship with the Táin as if it were just that, and to let the matter rest with the observation that both found in the Táin what they were looking for, selected those ingredients which matched their respective sensibilities and magnified them into a master image of the source text, the Rorschach text. The most important difference between Gregory and Kinsella is that one is anterior to the other. The latter-day Kinsella cannot approach the Táin directly: he stands at the further end of a whole tradition of Anglo-Irish approaches to the Táin, and cannot pretend that his forerunners never existed. Between the Gaelic Táin and Kinsella lie the filters of Lady Gregory and of the many authors inspired by her. These earlier Anglo-Irish renderings of the Táin in turn become parameters in a tradition which partly defines Kinsella's own position vis-à-vis his source text. Kinsella follows Gregory in what Jorge Luis Borges, when he discussed the successive translators of the Arabian Nights, called a "dynasty of enemies".

We can see that Kinsella tries to rid himself of the precedence of his forerunners. For one thing he decides to turn to a Gaelic version of the Táin which has been left relatively untouched by earlier translators; for Kinsella uses a different MS redaction of the old epic: not the Book of Leinster version which is the more unified narrative, but the more fragmented, earlier and less polished (and, hence, more appealing) version as written down in the Yellow Book of Lecan. Even so, Kinsella often finds himself forced to turn to the rationalized version of the Book of Leinster in order to make sense of the fragments related in his main source, the Yellow Book of Lecan.

But there is another principle at work here as well, which may be best illustrated with an anecdote. -- The third-century Latin geographer Solinus wrote an account of Ireland in which he stated, among other things, that that country harboured no snakes and no bees. The absence of snakes is indisputable; but later authors found that bees did occur in Ireland despite Solinus's claim to the contrary. Consequently, twelfth-century Giraldus Cambrensis and sixteenth-century Richard Stanyhurst took care to stress the presence of bees in Ireland; which in turn led later, seventeenth century authors like William Camden and Fynes Moryson (who seem to have read Cambrensis or Stanyhurst more attentively than the earlier Solinus) to assert that Ireland was remarkable both for the absence of snakes and for its plenitude of bees.[10]

This anecdote illustrates, I think, a mechanism of some significance in the transmission of imagotypical attitudes: namely, that an initial idea, once it has been formulated, may be inverted into its very opposite under the pressure of falsification or changes in outlook, but that one way or another its traces will remain operative, that it will be modified but cannot be ignored. Something similar is at work with Thomas Kinsella's version of the Táin. Kinsella's view of the primitive roughness of ancient Gaelic society is, I think, partly a result of his general poetic sensibility as it is expressed in *A Technical Supplement* or *Notes from the Land of the Dead,* a decidedly modernist and, as such, anti-romantic preoccupation with the human mind as it faces existence in a hostile universe; as such, Kinsella's image of ancient Gaelic Ireland[11] becomes largely definable as being about as unlike that of Lady Gregory as one can get; at the same time, we see that Kinsella's reaction against the Victorian starry-eyed romanticization of Ancient Ireland becomes meaningful in its own right, as a characteristic and even defining factor in his own imagery. In other words, Kinsella's image of Gaelic Ireland is materially circumscribed by his image of the Victorian image of Gaelic Ireland. If Lady Gregory said that there were no bees in Ireland, Kinsella says that there are swarms of them. If the hero of Lady Gregory's Táin is Cuchulain, and its heroines are ladylike and somewhat statuesque caryatides, Kinsella sees these latter as follows:

> Probably the greatest achievement of the *Táin* and the Ulster cycle is the series of women, some in full scale and some in miniature, on whose strong and diverse personalities the action continually turns: Medb, Derdriu, Macha, Nes, Aife. It may be as goddess-figures, ultimately, that these women have their power; it is certainly they, under all the violence, who remain most real in the memory (pp. xiv-xv).

Again, if Lady Gregory suppresses sex and excretion in her version of the Táin, Kinsella brings these matters into the foreground

---

[10] Cf. my own *Mere Irish & Fíor-Ghael. Studies in the Idea of Irish Nationality, its Development and Literary Expression prior to the Nineteenth Century* (Amsterdam/Philadelphia: John Benjamins, 1986), esp. pp. 34-5, 167.

[11] Much of Kinsella's poetry harks back to Gaelic mythography, as in the *Lebor Gabála* (e.g. the poems "Finistère" and "The Oldest Place", in *One and other Poems* (Dublin: Dolmen, 1979); echoes of his penchant for science fiction can also be recognized in the imagery which he weaves of that mysterious and disconcerting culture.

-- significantly, because he feels them to be linked to the Táin's characteristic brutality: they are "an effect of the same directness with which the story treats killing and mutilation" (p. xiv).

One of the most characteristic instances of such a process concerns an episode where Fergus sleeps with Medb. At this occasion, Medb's cuckolded husband Ailill has Fergus' sword stolen, and Fergus finds himself swordless, with an empty scabbard. He does not get his sword back until the final battle, and meanwhile has to make do with a wooden imitation sword. Kinsella reads this episode as follows:

> Their [Fergus' and Medb's] encounter in the wood, where Fergus (clearly not up to Medb's demands) loses his sword, is the source of continual phallic joking in the *Táin* until the sword is restored ... (p. xiv)

I do not want to deny that terms like "tool" or "weapon" have long been played upon in this manner; Shakespeare and the metaphysical poets abound with examples. However, the stealing of Fergus' sword is not all that obvious a symbol to me of his sexual inadequacy; and I feel that we should be aware that as post-Freudians we are more sensitive to such symbolism than ever before; anything is a phallic symbol to us provided it is longer than it is wide. It may be, therefore, that such a sexualization of the Táin, apart from its brief references to bodily functions, though it sets out to be a "restoration" of its true content after previous bowdlerizations, may in itself be an imagotypical projection of a contemporary outlook upon the original[12] -- an imagotypical projection which is, of course,

---

[12] A number of instances can be given where Kinsella's representation of sex and excretion appears to be given for its own sake rather than as the restitution of fidelity it pretends to be. I have selected three of them, and arranged them into the following synoptic scheme. This scheme illustrates, I think, the fact that Kinsella's "sexualization" of the Tain need by no means be reflective of a "reconstitution of fidelity to the source", as against Gregory's alleged bowdlerization. These examples illustrate the possibilities that LG's primmer version is a result of her having used a primmer MS redaction (first example); or that TK has to abandon his own preferred source in order to glean his pelvic matters elsewhere, in a breach of source fidelity (third example); or both (second example).

LG's SOURCE MS	LG	TK	TK's SOURCE MS
Medb offers golden brooch	Medb offers golden brooch	Medb offers friendly thighs	Medb offers friendly thighs
M. offers close friendship	M. offers close friendship	Medb offers friendly thighs	(EPISODE IS ABSENT)

counter to, and corrective of earlier ones, but a projection nevertheless.

Indeed there is plenty of phallic joking in Fergus' weaponry as described by Lady Gregory, for those who care to look for that sort of thing. In her version, though the tryst in the wood, the stealing of Fergus' sword and the wooden replica are all present, Fergus is never really swordless; his weapon lies in all its redoubtable length across his thighs when he goes in his chariot to parley with Cuchulain;[13] and, what is more, the wooden sword here takes on a completely different role, and becomes the envoy's white wooden wand which, like a white flag, is a sign for Cuchulain that Fergus is coming to him as an emissary rather than a challenger or enemy.

This in turn complicates matters even further. Not only can Kinsella's emphasis on the pelvic be shown to be a reaction against a previous interpretation as much as a rendering of what he sees in the original; not only do later versions of the Táin interact with each other as well as with their source; but it also appears that differences result from that very source itself as much as from the divergence between various later interpretations. The source itself turns out to be contradictory and heterogeneous; there is no such thing as a discrete entity called "the original". Indeed, "the original" of the Anglo-Irish tradition of Táin-translations is in itself just that: a tradition, with various redactions in different manuscripts, contradictory and full of different versions of the events narrated. "The original" itself is wrapped in paratextual coating after coating. There is, for instance, the injunction made by the compiler at the end of the Book of Leinster text, not to vary or change the version of the Táin which he has just finished relating:

M. menstruates and urinates	(EPISODE IS SUPPRESSED)	M. menstruates and urinates	(EPISODE IS ABSENT)

These examples are narrated, respectively, in: (A) CO'R pp. 72 & 212, also ed.'s note to ll. 86-7, p. 277; LG p. 174 and TK p. 169; (B) CO'R pp. 3 & 140; LG p. 143; TK p. 55; (C) CO'R pp. 133 & 269; LG p. 204; TK p. 250.
[13] LG p. 160, but cf. p. 170. Cf. also CO'R p. 182 who here collates different MSS into the phrase "A long sword, as long as a ship's rudder, firmly fixed and resting on the two thighs of the great, proud warrior who is within the chariot" (11. 1585-7 in the gaelic text, p. 43: "Claideb fata sithlaí co n-ecrasaib serrda for díb sliastaib sudigthi dond óclaíg móir borrfaid fail isin charput ar medón.")

> A blessing on every one who shall faithfully memorise the
> Táin as it is written here and shall not add any other form
> to it.[14]

Even here the volatility of "the" Táin as a textual tradition
rather than as a unitary story seems to be painfully obvious to the
compiler, and to cause him misgivings which in the light of the
present argument turn out to be only too justified; indeed his *n e
varietur* is immediately followed by a later scribal comment in Latin
which monkishly observes:

> But I who have written this story, or rather this fable,
> give no credence to the various incidents related in it. For
> some things in it are the deceptions of demons, others
> poetic figments; some are probable, others improbable;
> while still others are intended for the delectation of
> foolish men.[15]

And then, after one has penetrated through these scribal ironies
in "the original's" very own paratext, one finds a further, narrative
paratextuality in the notion of the *rémscéla*, the aforementioned
ancillary tales. One of these, significantly, concerns the *Dofallsigud
Tána Bó Cuailnge* or the "Retrieval of the Táin Bó Cuailnge". It relates
how knowledge of the Táin had almost vanished from the Irish
literati's memory, each poet of Ireland remembering only a small
portion of the narrative. Senchán Torpéist then sends his son and his
pupil to retrieve the full text of the Táin from the West, and the ghost
of Fergus himself, one of the protagonists, recites the story to them in
a kind of *aisling*-vision. "However", in Kinsella's wording,

> there are some who say that the story was told to Senchán
> himself after he had gone on a fast to certain saints of the
> seed of Fergus. This seems reasonable.[16]

---

[14] CO'R p. 272. In the original, p. 136 11. 4919-20: "Bendacht ar cech óen
mebraigfes go hindraic Táin amlaid seo & ná tuillfe cruth aile furri."

[15] CO'R p. 272. In the original, p. 136 11. 4921-5: "Sed ego qui scripsi hanc
historiam; aut verius fabulam quibusdam fidem in hac historia aut fabula non
accommodo. Quaedam enim ibi sunt praestrigia demonum, quaedam autem
figmenta poetica, quaedam similia vero, quaedam non, quaedam ad
delectationem stultorum." It will be noted that the scribe's use of the term
"similia vero" indicates, even at this early date, a critical shift towards reading
the Táin as literature rather than as historiography or even mythography: the
criticism being that, even as a tale, the Táin is a failure in that it breaks the
laws of verisimilitude / mimetic realism / *vraisemblance*.

[16] TK p. 2. In the original: "Asberat alaili imorro isdoSenchán adchaos
iartroscud frinoebu síl Fergus & nibo machthad cidsamlaid nobeth."
(*Zeitschrift für Vergleichende Sprachforschung* 28 (1887), 433-4.)

This anecdote dates from the ninth century. Even at that early date, there is already a highly troubled relationship between the text of the Táin, as a story, and the knowledge or historical/literary reference contained in it; the Táin is already a title covering a mystery or unknown quantity from the past, rather than a straightforward narrative. And not only does this brief story testify to a lack of unambiguous knowledge of past history; it even participates in such ambiguity, in that it gives two possible versions, not of the Táin itself, but (at one remove) of how it was retrieved.

Indeed, it becomes apparent that of the two redactions, the earlier one is the vaguer one, giving more variant versions of the individual episodes; so that the later Book of Leinster redaction appears as a deliberate *ex posteriori* unification of what must have been disparate and contradictory source traditions; and the "blessing on those who memorize the Táin without any divergence from this version" begins to sound less like an archaic invocation of the sacredness of the Tale than like a sigh of relief on the redactor's finally having unified the complex of contradictory Táin-stories. Thus, as one approaches "the original", the picture becomes scarcely less diffuse; and at the very heart of the oldest available core texts there are still those vaguenesses and ambiguities which will bedevil any attempt to seize, let alone to transmit, the pristine, primitive Original.

What is a tradition? I think the foregoing shows that it is less a discrete category working through history, than a unifying concern projected, *ex posteriori* and retroactively, on the contradictory multifariousness of the past and on its previous interpretations, an imposition of images upon images. The implication is that, in studying "traditions" like the Irish or Anglo-Irish ones, it would be wise to disregard their truth-claim, to avoid supposing or seeking an unambiguous historical reality behind the images against which they can be falsified or verified. Instead, one should perhaps choose to concentrate primarily on the how and the why, on the strategies and shaping desires, of such evocations, impositions, projections.

Joep Leerssen

THE ABBEY THEATRE AS A CULTURAL FORMATION

The purpose of this paper is theoretical, not historical. I would like to explore the usefulness of the concept of *cultural formation* - a newcomer in literary and cultural theory of the last decade - by applying it to a well-documented subject-matter, namely: the work of the Abbey Theatre playwrights (and players) in the first quarter of this century, up to, say, the production of Sean O'Casey's last play in the Dublin trilogy, *The Plough and the Stars* (1926). In doing so I hope to provide a few new emphases to the overall picture of the Abbey Theatre in its heyday.

"Cultural formation" is one of the key-concepts in Raymond Williams's theory of culture.[1] It is used, roughly, to refer to a group of artists, a tendency in art, a school, a movement, and the like. Examples: the pre-Raphaelite Brotherhood, Godwin and his circle, Bloomsbury, the international avant-garde, the Fabians, many of the so-called "isms", etc. The existence and interest of cultural formations is of course one of the most obvious phenomena for which a sociology of culture or of literature has to account. But the salient point in those accounts is precisely the *way* in which cultural formations are studied.

Before going into that, one may wonder whether the Abbey Theatre could be called a cultural formation in this pre-conceptual, empirical sense. I think the answer is yes. Yeats and a group of friends around him (Lady Gregory, John Synge, Douglas Hyde, Edward Martyn, George Moore, AE) are widely recognized as the pioneers of the Irish cultural revival, the centre of which was undisputably the Abbey Theatre. In his well-known *Ireland Since the Famine*, the historian F.S.L. Lyons speaks of Yeats's circle as "a quite small and closely-knit group who were exposed to certain very specific influences"[2]. Among these he lists: an interest in the occult, the magic, theosophy (especially AE and Yeats), the newly discovered old Irish sagas and fairy-tales (Yeats, Synge, Hyde, lady Gregory) and the figure of Parnell, blown into mythical proportions after his fall. He also mentions their common roots in the west of Ireland (which may explain their interest in the

---

[1] See esp. R. Williams, *Marxism and Literature* (Oxford: Oxford Univ. Press, 1977); *Culture* (London: Fontana Paperbacks, 1981) and *Problems in Materialism and Culture* (London: Verso, 1980).
[2] F.S.L. Lyons, *Ireland Since the Famine* (London: Fontana, 1973), p. 234 and pp. 234-236 passim.

peasant and his idiom) and their background as gentry of Anglo- Irish protestant stock (save for Yeats and AE who were from the professional middle-class, and for Martyn and Moore who were catholics). In the opinion of many, the most important contribution of this group of playwrights was the creation of the peasant or folk play[3]. Whether this is accurate or not, after the formative years of the Abbey the Dublin public began to rate each new play, ironically, by its PQ (peasant quality)[4], and such plays or dramatic dialogue came to be known as "typical Abbey". Brendan Behan, born in 1923, must have seen so many of them that, as he remembers in *Borstal Boy*:

> At home on the corner of the North Circular Rd we used to make a jeer of that Abbey Theatre bogman talk: "Oh woman of the roads, be not putting it on me now! With your long arm, and your strong arm, be after pulling me a pint of porther.[5]

Parody seems to be the surest sign of a style that has caught on. Already in 1909 Gerald MacNamara gave a parody of Synge's peasant speech:

> Clarence: And you think, kind ladies, that I have the gift of   the bards upon me?
> Cissie: Sure, it's as plain to be seen as the staff of a pike, for the beautiful words pour from your lips like a delf jug, and it full of buttermilk.
> (from: *The Mist That does Be On the Bog*)

Yet it would be erroneous, I think, to identify the Abbey Theatre as a whole, even in its earlier period, with the kind of dialogue parodied here, or, more generally, with the peasant play. But that there was something like an Abbey "stamp" seems undeniable.

So let us return to our concept. The point, as I said, is how to find the proper way to study cultural formations, in other words, how to make formational analysis function in a wider analytical framework. Not everybody seems convinced of the necessity of this systematic approach. There are those who prefer to stress the individuality of each artist. Michea'l O' hAodha, writing about John Synge in his *Theatre in Ireland*, is a case in point:

---

3 See e.g. M. O hAodha, *Theatre in Ireland*, Blackwell, Oxford, 1974. O hAodha considers the peasant play as "the one distinctive strain which Ireland has contributed to world drama" (p.XII).

4 See Lyons, op. cit., p. 235.

5 B. Behan, *Borstal Boy* (London: Corgi Books, 1958), p. 106.

Nationality like parentage, family, education and vocation, is something one cannot escape. Synge came closely in touch with nationalism, became an unbeliever, lived in the cabins of the Irish-speaking peasantry but he cannot be said to be representative of anybody or anything. He was, in fact, nothing but an artist.[6]

Others acknowledge the significance of cultural groups, movements, schools, etc., but attempt to account for them in terms of idealistic constructions, such as: national, literary or artistic traditions, histories of ideas, psychological models, spiritual archetypes, etc.

What Williams has in mind in proposing his term, is an analysis of cultural groups that is fully integrated into a general and dynamic theory of culture (dynamic in the sense that it studies structures as processes). *Culture*, for him, is "a signifying system through which necessarily (though among other means) a social order is communicated, reproduced, experienced and explored"[7]. In his view, a ruling class asserts its *hegemony* (its power) by imposing a dominant culture and an effective social order. A *dominant culture* is created by selecting from *tradition* those works, meanings and values that may help to preserve the interests of the ruling class. The most effective instruments to that end are identifiable *institutions* (family, schools, churches, places of work, the media), which serve to preselect and impose meanings, values, opinions, etc. upon us. But the establishment of a dominant culture also depends on *formations*, i.e. conscious movements and tendencies in artistic and intellectual life, which often have variable and oblique relations to formal institutions, sometimes even positively contrasting ones, and which mostly resist reduction to some generalized hegemonic function. With regard to the dominant culture, formations may indeed be *alternative* or downright *oppositional*, the former when association is based on dissent from and implicit criticism of the dominant culture, the latter when the formation mounts an open attack on available art forms, institutions and the general conditions that sustain them.[8] The members of the formation need not be, and mostly are not conscious of these oppositional or alternative positions.

All these concepts can be made operational in what Williams calls formational analysis. In such an analysis one should not only provide a careful description of the ideology (conscious meanings and values) of a particular group or movement, but also transcend this description

---

6 O hAodha, op. cit., p. 42.

7 *Culture*, op. cit., p. 13.

8 ibid., chapter 3, passim.

by putting sociological questions to general history.   One should also
attend to individual differences inside the group, so as to show how
diverse positions, interests and influences of individuals are resolved
by the formations, whereas others remain as internal tensions, often as
the ground for subsequent break-aways (the history of the Abbey
Theatre offers a few striking cases in point).   The study of these
individual differences necessarily involves attention to literary forms.[9]

Let me now try to formulate the questions with which I am
concerned in terms of the theory just sketched. 1. How can we define
the ethos of the Abbey Theatre as a cultural formation from the
accounts given by the group itself (i.e. the group as it sees itself),
especially in its relation to the theatre as an institution?   2. In what
relationship did the formation stand to tradition and the dominant
culture (did it give voice to the values of the ruling class, was it
alternative, oppositional)?   This is the analysis of the implied meanings
and the values taken for granted.   It transcends the ideological horizon
of the group itself by projecting it against the background of general
history.   3. How did the forms of the Abbey plays help to shape and
enact the formation?   This is where formational analysis links up with
the analysis of literary forms of individual works.

The Formation Of the Abbey Theatre

We must first decide whom to include into the cultural formation
of the Abbey Theatre.   To the list of intimates of the Yeats circle
mentioned before, one name should be added, that of Sean O'Casey,
who, as I shall argue, came so close to the Yeats group in mentality and
aesthetic convictions (at least for a time), that he may rightly be
considered as belonging to the formation.   Other names may be
crossed: Edward Martyn, Douglas Hyde, George Moore and AE.   Martyn
broke away early from the Abbey and became an ardent nationalist;
Douglas Hyde wrote his plays in Gaelic, and unlike Yeats and the
others, he promoted Irish literature in Gaelic; George Moore, after a
few none too successful attempts at collaboration, soom disappeared
"from the stage"; and AE's contribution to the theatre was negligible.

As for the majority of the Abbey Theatre playwrights, they
cannot really be said to belong to the Abbey Theatre *formation*.   They
were part of the *institution*, together with the patriotic middle-class
audience, the critics, the financiers, the state, possibly even the censor.
But the writers of the Yeats group differed from the institution, to
which they had given rise, on so many issues, that they repeatedly
became the butt of public outcry (cf. the rows).   Eventually - as Yeats

---

[9] ibid., pp. 85-86.

had to acknowledge in a sad note of resignation in 1919[10] - they had to yield their dominant position to the nationalist group. If one discounts the O'Casey period in the early twenties, which made the Abbey veer round again to its early ideals, the patriotic middle-class public was in general triumphant in seeing its values embodied and consecrated in the host of peasant or small country town plays of the Colum or Cork Realists type of the second decade of the century.[11] Those values might serve to define the Yeats formation negatively: an ardent patriotism, a central concern with the Irish peasantry and what it embodied: catholicism and love of the land, and a view of art as propaganda (the Abbey Theatre was *their* national theatre, and they saw it not only as an instrument of cultural, but also political emancipation).[12]

Yeats and his friends were dissenters in all these domains. They were nationalists, certainly, but their nationalism had a cosmopolitan flavour, as opposed to that of their middle-class opponents Arthur Griffith, D.P.Moran and others, for whom "the Gael" (catholic, Irish speaking, virulently anti-British) was the centre of all things Irish. Yeats, Synge and Lady Gregory had, each to a varying extent, alienated themselves from their class, the Anglo-Irish Ascendancy. But for all their efforts to unite with the Irish in the creation of the Celtic Revival, their wider social and cultural background would always prevent their full immersion into Gaelic civilization. Their conscious effort was thus directed to the fusion of the two cultures, for example by creating an Irish literature in English. Although they supported the Gaelic League, not just for its spirit of tolerance and collaboration between all parties

---

10 "Yet we did not set out to create this sort of theatre, and its success has been to me a discouragement and a defeat", W.B. Yeats, "A People's Theatre", *The Irish Statesman*, Autumn 1919, reprinted in A.N. Jeffares (ed.), *Yeats, Selected Criticism* (London: MacMillan, 1970), p. 186.

11 The Cork Realists were L. Robinson, T.C. Murray and R.J. Ray. Other playwrights in this tradition are W. Boyle, St. John Ervine, S. O'Kelly and many others, some of them talented (Robinson, Murray), others sometimes pretty vulgar. They may occasionally come up to the standards of a Synge or O'Casey play, as in G. Fitzmaurice's *The Pie-dish* or P. Colum's *The Fiddler's House*.

12 These meanings and values are indeed rough approximations of what were in reality critical and often conflicting positions. But at all levels of the institution (audience, press, actors, playwrights and, perhaps least of all, the board of directors) patriotism seems to have been the norm and a lapse of patriotic criticism was Arthur Griffith's review of Synge's *In the Shadow of the Glen* in 1903. The butt of his critique was in fact Yeats, who had defended Synge: "Mr Yeats does not give any reason why if the Irish National Theatre has now no propaganda save that of good art, it should continue to call itself either Irish or National. If the Theatre be solely an Art Theatre, then its plays can fairly be criticized from the standpoint of art. But whilst it calls itself Irish National, its productions must be considered and criticized as Irish National productions" (*United Irishman*, 24 October 1903, quoted in F.S.L. Lyons, *Culture and Anarchy in Ireland 1890-1939* (Clarendon Press: Oxford, 1979), p. 68.)

and sections, but also for its revival of the old Irish tongue[13], and were drawing on Irish dialects for poetic inspiration themselves, they still regarded the English language as the sole instrument apt to make Ireland join Europe. As regards O'Casey's nationalism, although it had gone through a different evolution from that of Yeats, Synge and Lady Gregory, it turned out in the end to be just as open and cosmopolitan as theirs. He, for one, did make an attempt to become fully immersed in Irish nationalism. But it failed, as did his subsequent attempt to get involved with proletarian action when acting as secretary in Jim Larkin's Irish Citizen Army. At the time when O'Casey began to write plays for the Abbey, his nationalism was as far removed from middle-class patriotism as that of Yeats or Synge a decade or so earlier. His cosmopolitanism was soon to declare itself, when he decided, like Joyce, to turn his back on Ireland for good, "a voluntary and settled exile from every creed, from every party"[14]. So the common political ground between Yeats, Synge and O'Casey is really their contempt of middle-class patriotism (O'Casey spoke of "theocracy", Yeats of "the throng", Synge of "the sweaty-headed swine"). Yeats could still detect at times a strain of heroism in those people (as in 1916), but O'Casey refused to see even that: he saw the Rising as a mistake and could only feel sympathy with the non-combatants.

With respect to Ireland's future, their political ideas were rather utopian, though not uninteresting. They felt it their task to awaken the country to its spiritual richness. For Yeats, this mostly carried mystical overtones. Yet he often championed the cause of a tolerant, mature, a-clerical and culturally emancipated Ireland. His "divorce speech" and his efforts to bring back the Hugh Lane pictures to Ireland are cases in point. But till the end of his life he would disdain party politics, and as he grew older, his elitist beliefs in a few able men to lead the country grew stronger. The Ireland that Synge dreamed of was hardly more realisable than Yeats's since it was modelled on a form of pre- colonial communal life that he had found on the Aran Islands, where people lived close to nature, where social life knew no division of labour and was free from narrow class conventions. As for O'Casey, after retiring from politics, he only desired and hoped, as Lady Gregory wrote, to lead the workers into "a better life, an interest in reading, in drama especially".[15] "Trade Unionism, he said, may give the worker a larger dinnerplate - which, heaven knows, he badly needs - but it will never

---

[13] Support was not always unwavering. In his "Letter To the Gaelic League" Synge lashes out against "the incoherent twaddle passed off as Irish" by the Gaelic League and attacks its "wilful nationalism" (see R. skelton, *The Writings of J.M. Synge* (London: Thames and Hudson, 1971), p. 107.

[14] Sean O'Casey, *Autobiographies II*, MacMillan, London, 1963, p. 231.

[15] Lady Gregory, *Journals*, in T. Kilroy (ed.), *Sean O'Casey, A Collection of Critical Essays* (Englewood Cliffs, New Jersey: Prentice Hall, 1975), p. 20.

give him a broader mind, which he needs more badly still".[16] His model of working-class action was Jim Darkin, "a man who would put a flower in a vase as well as a loaf on a plate".[17]

The mitigated nationalism that characterizes the playwrights of the Abbey Theatre formation went not unexpectedly with their sympathy for the social class that was least affected by middle-class patriotism: Synge's, and to a lesser extent Yeats's "peasants" and Sean O'Casey's Dublin slum dwellers. These, however, were not the people written about in the average Abbey play. There we come across the socially mobile class of Irish peasants and country people after the Land War, in their climb through emigration and gradual urbanization, towards a rapidly growing new middle-class of petits bourgeois, middlemen, importers, small manufacturers, etc. Sean O'Faolain portrays them as follows:

> They were ordinary, decent, kindly, self-seeking men who had no intention of jeopardising their mushroom-prosperity by gratuitous display of moral courage. In any case, since they were rising to sudden wealth behind protective tariff-walls, they had a vested interest in nationalism and even in isolationism. The upshot of it was a holy alliance between the Church, the new businessmen, and the politicians.[18]

The people in the plays of the Yeats formation were not the social climbers that were to benefit by patriotism or revolution. They were either a stage behind it (as in Synge), or beyond it (Yeats), or they were its victims (O'Casey). They cannot even properly be called working-class.[19] Some of them are peasants or fishermen, but in Synge, and partly in Yeats, they are not quite the exploited Irish peasantry that we associate with colonial times. Yeats's and Synge's plays depend, as Thomas Kilroy says, "on the survival of a peasant culture with folk roots stretching deep into a heroic past".[20] But the characters in their plays are hard to classify socially. All those beggars, fools, cripples, vagrants, tramps, tinkers, pedlars, poachers, pirates, sailors, adventurers, poteen-makers, herds, ballad-singers, etc.

---

[16] Quoted by H. Coston, "Prelude to playwriting", in R. Ayling (ed.), *Sean O'Casey, Modern Judgements*, (London: MacMillan, 1969), p. 50.

[17] Lyons, 1973, op. cit., p. 276.

[18] Cf. J. Lindsay, "Sean O'Casey as a Socialist Artist", in R. Ayling, op. cit., p. 194.

[19] The Abbey Theatre as a whole may well have been "a people's theatre" (Yeats) in that it extended the range of appropriate subjects for dramatic expression to vast regions of the Irish population that hitherto had no voice in the theatre (Yeats's "dumb classes, each with its own knowledge of the world"). Among these the socially mobile countrymen loom very large. But in the plays of the Yeats formation this group is characteristically absent.

[20] Kilroy, op. cit., p. 2.

are in fact remnants of a pre-capitalist social order (we would now call them "marginals", "dropouts", "fourth world", etc.). Likewise in O'Casey we get what Jack Lindsay describes as "an odd mixture of working-class proper, lumpen-proletariat, and peasants in various stages of urban absorption".[21] O'Casey himself likes to refer to them as his "rags and tatters", "the knights of the pick and shovel", etc. What many of these characters (in O'Casey as well as in Yeats and Synge) have in common is a tragi-comic sense of life. They also often have a bit of anarchic blood in their veins, which is perhaps why they are usually followed with a benevolently critical eye by their authors. Yeats's program was to show both "the flower and the weed"[22], Synge was more interested in "the law-breaker than in the law-maker"[23] and O'Casey's "heroes" are in fact cowards, opportunists or even looters.

But the real working-class issues (Land War, evictions, famine, emigration) are either absent from these plays, or not central to them (with a few exceptions), or, when they are, as in O'Casey's Dublin trilogy, our interest is not with the protagonists of these events, but with "the ignorant and poor Dublin tenement dwellers bewilderingly caught up in these events".[24] An Irish Hauptmann is not to be found among the playwrights of the Yeats formation.[25]

Was this shift of focus due to ignorance about the vital working-class issues or failure to respond to them? Obviously not for O'Casey. Synge knew about the condition of the poor in the depressed areas of Ireland (Connemara, Mayo), as one can see from a series of articles he wrote about them for the Manchester Guardian. Besides that, he showed a lifelong interest in the way of life of the country people. Finally, Yeats was always more interested in the Irish peasant as a literary symbol. Yet, if we are to believe O'Casey, "Yeats, in his own peculiar way, loved the common people more than Griffith, MacNeill or de Valera did, or even could".[26] For all his aristocratic aloofness, he welcomed land purchase, supported the cooperative movement and the

---

[21] Ayling, op. cit., p. 193.

[22] See S.B.Bushrui (ed), *Sunshine & the Moon's Delight, A Centenary Tribute to J.M. Synge*, Irish Writers Series (Lewisburg: Bucknell University Press, 1972), p. 194 (article: "Synge and Yeats").

[23] Richard M. Kain, "The *Playboy* Riots", in Bushrui, op. cit. p. 175.

[24] See H. Goldstone, *In Search of Community: The Achievement of Sean O'Casey* (Dublin: The Mercier Press, Dublin, 1972), p. 23.

[25] I mean that in the period under review the Abbey Theatre formation did not produce a fully naturalistic play like Hauptmann's *The Weavers*, where the working-class is the protagonist in a specifically working-class issue: a social upheaval. It was not until much later that O'Casey would successfully tackle a real working-class issue from within, in *Red Roses for Me*, on the Larkin strike of 1913.

[26] See E. Cullinford, *Yeats, Ireland and Fascism* (MacMillan, London, 1981), p. 73.

revival of Irish industries and spoke out frankly against the lock-out of Irish workers in 1913. Time and again he found himself at odds with his own class, the Anglo-Irish Ascendancy, but - always an incendiary - revised his position when the Anglo-Irish had become virtually powerless themselves in the early years of the Irish Free State.[27]

If ignorance or lack of commitment cannot explain the relative absence or the highly idiosyncratic view of the real problems of the Irish working-class in the plays we are concerned with, there must be other reasons. The most important of these, I think, is the view of these playwrights on the autonomy of art. The Irish literary revival is often explained as a kind of literary Parnellism[28], the idea being that the deadlock in nationalist policies caused by the death of Parnell had shifted the struggle for emancipation from politics to culture. This meant that art would have to play an ancillary role: it would be a weapon in the struggle to forge a national Irish consciousness (Gaelic, catholic and rural), it would have to be patriotic, i.e. utilitarian and propagandistic. Even Yeats and Lady Gregory had to don a green bonnet in the theatre on one or two occasions.[29] But their natural tendency was to defend the freedom of the artist and the independence of the theatre tooth and nail. Yeats in particular always had a somewhat elitist conception of (especially his own) dramatic art. Although he wrote a few popular plays as well, his real interest was in creating "an unpopular theatre and an audience like a secret society where admission is by favour and never too many".[30] The effect he wanted to achieve, especially in his "closet plays", was not to make his audience change their political opinions, but to make them conscious of deep emotions through the medium of his poetically organized heroic and mythic material, "to pass for a few moments into the deep of the mind that had hitherto been too subtle for our habitation".[31] Yeats was a dreamer at some distance from reality, but always "leaning out to it". His realism is, however, well-hidden from view.

Synge could have written naturalist plays had he wanted to. Except for *Deirdre* and perhaps *The Well Of the Saints*, all his plays are firmly rooted in the real world. Yet, not unlike Yeats (but starting from the other end), he went beyond naturalism, firstly by limiting his scope to the remote, elemental world of the west of Ireland, secondly

---

[27] ibid., passim, esp. chapter 5, "Ideas of class".

[28] Lyons, 1973, op. cit., p.236; Yeats in Jeffares, op. cit., p. 195.

[29] P. Colum, W. Boyle, T. MacDonagh, S. O'Kelly, G. Shiels, T. MacSwiney, E. Martyn and others all wrote at least one orthodox patriotic play. So did Lady Gregory with *The Rising of the Moon* and Yeats with *Cathleen Ni Houlihan*.

[30] Yeats in Jeffares, op. cit., p. 190.

[31] See U. Ellis-Fermor, *The Irish Dramatic Movement* (London: Methuen, 1954), p. 90.

by giving a realistic and recognizable picture of this world, but then lifting it out of reality into a world of imagined possibilities. His people are rooted in "the clay and worms", but are "shying clods again the visage of the stars".[32] Synge disliked Ibsen (not quite deservedly) and the intellectual problem play: "The drama, he said, like the symphony, does not teach or prove anything, it gives the nourishment (...) on which our imaginations live".[33] His plays are indeed full of characters with impossible dreams that interfere with their actions, thus creating new tensions.[34] He was convinced that only people living on the fringe of society or on the seamy side of life can dream those dreams, and that it takes a poet with the soul of a vagrant to record them and make them live.

O'Casey's plays certainly move closer to the social and political issues of his time than those of Synge and Yeats. Yet he was far from being a propagandist. In a letter to Lady Gregory he criticizes a play by Upton Sinclair, because it only shows the suffering of the workers and not the conditions that arrest human development, namely "Stifling the desire, & destroying the power of creation, and deadening the faculty of understand and enjoy the higher things in life. To me the play is to Labour what street preaching is to religion...".[35] That he set great store by the aesthetic ideals of the Abbey Theatre formation can be seen from the near-religious awe with which he talks about it. He "worships" it[36], he speaks about Art and Literature (in capitals) as "the mantle and mirror of the Holy Ghost, and the sword of the Spirit". They are worth fighting for "with the last atom of strength", because they are "above and before all governments and parties".[37] He sees the theatre ecstatically as a place "beyond", somewhere where class differences are smoothed over and all work together for a better Ireland: "Aristocrats, middle-class and worker: Three in one and one in three".[38] He understands that the condition and ordeal of being a writer is to be an observer, "neither in it nor out of it"[39], and that art has more to do with self-realization than with class-consciousness.[40]

---

[32] Old Mahon in *The Playboy*, quoted by Ann Saddlemyer in R. Hogan (ed.), *The MacMillan Dictionary of Irish Literature* (London: MacMillan, 1980), p. 657.

[33] Preface to J.M. Synge, *The Tinkers's Wedding* in A. Saddlemyer (ed.), J.M. Synge, *Plays* (Oxford: Oxford University Press, 1969), p. 33.

[34] A. Saddlemyer in Hogan, op. cit., p. 657.

[35] David Krause, "A Self-Portrait of the Artist as a Man", in Ayling, op. cit., p. 243.

[36] ibid. p. 240.

[37] ibid. p. 247.

[38] ibid. p. 243.

[39] O'Casey, *Autobiographies II*, op. cit., p. 155.

[40] H. Coston in Ayling, op. cit., p. 50. O'Casey did not and would not always stick to that belief, because he never managed, nor perhaps wanted to ban out the socialist in him. The split with Yeats over *The Silver Tassie* was more or less predictable.

His plays, and especially his Dublin trilogy, are quite in tune with these beliefs. They never invite simple answers or reactions to individual problems or public causes, but always try to make us see, understand and sympathize. It is at this level that O'Casey joins Yeats and Synge.

Let me summarize the foregoing. The first (descriptive) phase of this formational analysis was meant to show that the inner core of the Abbey Theatre playwrights can quite clearly be set apart from the others in three important respects: their nationalism was cosmopolitan and cultural, not narrowly patriotic; their main interest went to common people living on the fringe of society, rather than to the mobile group that was rapidly forming a lower middle-class of native stock; finally they took art and literature as values in themselves, as creations of the imagination that give joy, rather than as means to a political end. It should be stressed that these conceptions and beliefs were quite consciously present with the group of writers we are discussing and that they constituted the cement that held it together. In the next stage of formational analysis I would like to transcend this conscious ideological horizon by studying the implied meanings and the values taken for granted and their relation to tradition and the dominant culture. It is here that the link with general history can be established.

The Abbey Theatre Formation As Cultural Vanguard

It is often difficult to see how culture and general history interconnect at a time when a social order is breaking up. In the period under review the class structure of Irish society was fundamentally changing. The Anglo-Irish ruling class was on the way out. Its decline had begun with the disestablishment of the Church of Ireland in 1869, and the situation deteriorated rapidly through a succession of events like "the Land War, Gladstone's legislation of 1881 making the tenant a partner in the soil with the landlord, the growth of land purchase under subsequent Tory governments, the coming of the country councils in 1898, above all the adoption of Home Rule as official Liberal policy" (F.S.L. Lyons, 1973).[41] As the star of Protestant Ascendancy was waning, that of the nationalist and catholic middle-class was rising (ibid.).[42] By the end of the period at study (1926) the reversal in the power structure had become a fact.

It seems clear from the start that the values and beliefs of the Abbey Theatre formation could not be fully endorsed by the old nor the new ruling class. In the last decade of the 19th century the Anglo-

---

[41] op. cit., p. 233.
[42] ibid., p. 244.

Irish were beginning to realize that the British way of life, which the Irish, especially the urban middle-class, had avidly adopted, was successfully challenged by emancipatory cultural movements, such as: the Gaelic League, the Gaelic Athletic Association and the early literary movements. The Abbey Theatre itself owed its origin to these movements and drew its strength and support from them, especially in its formative period before 1904. A point of extreme importance is that all, or nearly all of these emancipatory movements were started and led by Anglo-Irish dissidents. They were among the first to realize that their class had had its day and that the idea of a fusion of the two cultures, which we have mentioned earlier, was perhaps the best way to come to terms with the new situation. "This idea, says F.S.L. Lyons, should not be attributed to a death-bed repentance on the part of the entire Anglo-Irish Ascendancy (...) most of them - landlords and middle-class alike - remained serenely wedded to their traditional life-style, as loyal as ever to the Union, and as blind to Irish Ireland as if it had never existed".[43] On the other side of the political spectrum, the catholic middle-class was equally hostile to the idea of fusion. They were particularly against those Anglo-Irish who sought to involve themselves in the life of the country (one of their main targets was to break the influence of the Yeats group at the Abbey).

Sandwiched between two classes that both rejected them, the playwrights of the Yeats circle found themselves in a position which is rather difficult to assess in terms of subsequent developments. An analysis in crude class terms does not seem to carry us very far, since it is hard to say to which class these writers actually belonged. We might of course consider the Abbey Theatre formation as the forerunner of the consciousness of yet another new class in the making, but goodness knows what class.

Raymond Williams has coined the terms *residual* and *emergent*, to be applied to elements of the cultural process that are undeniably present, but cannot be reduced to the dominant cultural process. The residual is different from the "archaic" in that the residual is still active in the cultural process. Both residual and emergent elements may have an *alternative* or even *oppositional* relation to the dominant culture or may be wholly or largely *incorporated*. In contemporary culture organized religion, the idea of a rural community, or the monarchy are examples of residual cultural elements. The residual is primarily located in some earlier socio-cultural formation. For the emergent, this social basis is harder to define: it may, or may not be

---

[43] ibid., p. 234.

the formation of a new class, for there is a considerable amount of experience, in Williams's view, that is hard to describe in class terms.[44]

In their plays and their general comments on Irish culture and politics the playwrights of the Abbey Theatre formation show an odd mixture of residual and emergent elements, so that it is often very hard to disentangle them. Moreover, the varying ideological positions of each individual writer are not such as to reduce the complexity of the overall picture.

The most outspoken residual element in Yeats, Synge and Lady Gregory is the alliance between the aristrocrat and the peasant ("the noble and the beggarman") against the middle-class philistine. There is, I believe, no need to labour this point, which is virtually a truism. But the idea was not entirely alien to O'Casey either - and that certainly calls for an explanation. One should not forget that O'Casey was born into a Protestant middle-class family, albeit an impoverished one. Padraic Colum points out that the poor Protestants of the Dublin tenements felt like "a minority whithin a minority". They were "loyalists" and had pride in being part of an "Ascendancy". They cultivated an exclusiveness. So did O'Casey, and by asserting this Colum does not mean to belittle his commitment to Irish causes.[45] But the exclusiveness remained, which can be seen from the admiring pages O'Casey dedicates to lady Gregory (and Yeats) when he is received at Coole. After telling us that he and the Old lady "got on grand together", he wonders "how she of the grandees had managed to come so close to the common people".[46] He admires her when she speaks "warm words to the ploughman", sings songs with the people and mourns with them. "The taste of rare wine mingled with that of home-made bread on the tip of her tongue; her finely-shod feet felt the true warmth of the turf fire, and beside its glow she often emptied the sorrows of her own heart into the sorrow of others. Out of her plush and plum she came to serve the people, body and mind, with whatever faculties God had given her".[47] When reading this text, which was written in 1949, one feels as if the spirit of Yeats had moved O'Casey into this eulogy of a feudal age. Later, when he laments the destruction of Coole by the Irish government, it is as if we hear Yeats himself: "Oh! a scurvy act for an Irish government to do on the memory of one who was greater than the whole bunch of them put together and tied with a string. The god-damned Philistines".[48] One

---

44 Williams, Marxism and Literature, op. cit., pp. 121-127.
45 P. Colum, "Sean O'Casey's Narratives", in Ayling, op. cit., pp. 225-226.
46 O'Casey, *Autobiographies II*, op. cit., p. 111.
47 ibid., p. 113.
48 ibid., p. 125.

may feel that O'Casey is speaking with a borrowed accent here and that he feels on much surer ground when he can move among the Dublin tenements. Perhaps his greatly longed for admission into the inner core of Abbey Theatre playwrights and the hostile reception of some of his plays by the catholic and nationalist middle-class audience obstructed his view for a while and made him espouse a kind of Yeatsian "aristrocatic populism".[49]

However that may be, the idealization of the peasant and his assimilation with the aristocrat (and the artist) was definitely a residual element which retains an oppositional flavour. It offended the emerging Gaelic and Catholic middle-class. The reason for that may have been, in the opinion of Conor Cruise O'Brien, that "The natives they (Synge and Yeats) idealized were those who had remained most thoroughly native: and unfortunately they idealized these in ways that did not appear to the Catholic *colonisés* to be ideal".[50] They felt, in fact, as Micheál O' hAodha says, that "the noble peasant" had supplanted "the stage Irishman".[51]

Next to the element of the noble peasant, and related to it, there were some other residual elements in the Yeats formation: a bardic conception of literature (the poet as castigator and prophet)[52], a kind of Cobbettian anti-urban and anti-industrial view of nature, and a dislike of democracy (especially in Yeats and Synge, but for different reasons).[53] These elements are less central to the formation as a whole, because they apply to the works of the different playwrights rather unevenly and often exist side by side, in an uneasy tension, with emergent elements (for example, Yeats's defence of particular working-class and liberal issues as opposed to his authoritarianism).

The emergent elements reveal more about the essence of the Abbey Theatre formation than the residual ones. After all, the Abbey as Yeats, Synge, Lady Gregory and O'Casey saw it was an emancipation movement, based on the dual rejection of the old colonial order and the claims for power of the new catholic middle-class. Did these writers have an alternative to the social order they rejected? Their views are certainly divergent here, but there are important elements that overlap.

---

49 The term is E. Cullingford's.

50 C.C. O'Brien, *States of Ireland*, Hutchinson of London, 1972, p. 73.

51 O hAodha, op. cit., p. 52.

52 One may think of Yeats's *The King's Threshold* and Synge's *The Well of the Saints*.

53 The streak of authoritarianism in Yeats is well-documented (see notes 57 and 58); Synge was not against political democracy as such, but he felt it reduced everything to middle-class mediocrity.

In Synge there is an unresolved tension between his deep personal and artistic involvement with the communal, almost classless, but definitely residual way of life of the Aran Islands (which is also that of *Riders To the Sea*) and the extremely modern sensibility that permeates plays like *The Tinker's Wedding*, *The Shadow of the Glen*, *The Well Of the Saints* and *The Playboy Of the Western World*. If solidarity and courage are the elements that keep the people of the Aran Islands together, in the other plays, on the contrary, it is an almost anarchic spirit of individualism and liberty that holds sway. As Robin Skelton says, the characters in these plays reject "the constricting uniformity of orthodox social attitudes. He (Synge) is claiming liberty of action for the individual man and opposing any authority, ecclesiastic or political".[54]   He is opposed to capitalist democracy because it degrades people to selling their "birthright for a mess of pottage".[55]   Not that he is hankering, like Yeats, after a form of 18th century enlightened authoritarianism.   Rather, he wants to increase the liberty of the ididival, which includes the liberty to reject bourgeois conventions of property and morality and to opt out of modern urban civilization.[56]   Synge was not accepted nor understood by the Irish audiences of his time.   His work was truly oppositional, and is not yet fully incorporated, I think, at least not in Ireland.   *The Tinker's Wedding* got its first performance at the Abbey only in 1971. Since there was, nor is, as yet, a solid social basis for his utopian dream, one cannot say that, even in more permissive societies, his work has lost its appeal.   However, the danger of incorporation "as idealization or fantasy, or as an exotic - residential or escape - leisure function of the dominant order itself"[57] is particularly great with an *oeuvre* that, like Synge's, and for all its charm, lacks the necessary political coherence to oppose the baseness and aridness of a materialistic society with something more than the anarchic "song" of a marginal.   Synge's message is still alternative, even outside Ireland, but it would take a great director to make it oppositional again.

Yeats's anarchy is not that of the dropout, but of Lord Byron.   It is the Cuchullain-like freedom of the artist, and by extension, of the educated and ablest men to do as they like and to define their own responsibilities.   In his well-known article "Passion and Cunning: Notes On the Politics of W.B.Yeats"[58], Conor Cruise O'Brien attempts to define the limits of Yeats's notion of freedom:

---

54   See R. Skelton, *J. M. Synge*, p. 56.
55   Skelton, op.cit., p. 54
56   ibid. pp. 79 and 112.
57   Williams, *Marxism and Literature*, op.cit., p. 122.
58   C.C.O'Brien in W.H.Pritchard (ed.), *W.B.Yeats* (London: Harmondsworth, 1972), p. 331.

> He defended the liberty of the artist, consistently. In politics (...) he defended the liberty of Ireland against English domination, and the liberty of his own caste - and sometimes, by extension, of others - against clerical domination. Often these liberties overlapped, and the cause of artist and aristocrat became the same; often his resistance to "clerical" authoritarianism (his position on the lock-out, on divorce, on censorship) makes him appear a liberal. But his objection to clerical authoritarianism is not the liberal's objection to *all* authoritarianism. On the contrary he favours "a despotism of the educated classes" and in the search for this, is drawn towards fascism.

In a reply to O'Brien, entitled *Yeats, Ireland and Fascism*, Elisabeth Cullingford admits all the facts about Yeats's involvement with Irish fascism, but she calls it a brief aberration. She shows fairly convincingly, I think, that Yeats's long-term goal was "the rule of the educated, an aristocratic party organization based on the model of the family"[59]. If we accept this redefinition, Yeats's notion of freedom seems to be largely tributary to 19th century bourgeois liberalism (national independence, curtailment of the tyranny of the clergy) and romanticism (freedom of the artist). In the Ireland of his time, however, these elements were undoubtedly emergent, one of them even downright oppositional: anticlericalism. Even today this element does not seem to have lost its oppositional edge in Ireland. Another element that has consistently been rejected is the idea of a new Ireland, born out of the fusion of the two cultures. In *The Words Upon the Window Pane* (1930) Yeats seems to admit (and regret) his failure to bring about the Ireland he had dreamed of. He and his friends had lived on the false assumption that collaboration between classes, religions and races could be possible in a politically divided Ireland.[60] The idea of fusion may live on, however, as long as its opposite (Yeats would say its "mask") can only produce political deadlock and civil war, as we see in Northern Ireland today. Against the backdrop of this contemporary crisis a play like Yeats's *The Dreaming Of the Bones* (written in 1917, but first performed in 1931) has lost nothing of its relevance.

In O'Casey's plays, finally, and especially in the Dublin trilogy, the critique of middle-class patriotism and clericalism reached the limits of what the Abbey Theatre formation could accommodate. O'Casey is the only one who could have gone beyond a radical middle-class critique of a middle-class issue. But he did not, at least not in the Dublin trilogy.

---

[59] Cullingford, op.cit., p. 212.
[60] Cf. Lyons, 1973, op.cit., p. 246.

There he stopped short at the point where the uncompromisingly emergent elements could have appeared. The Dublin trilogy of course displays an embryonic working-class consciousness, in that it clearly shows that the poor of the Dublin tenements have nothing to gain by a patriotic unprising a war with the British or a civil war (apart from what they can loot). They are fighting someone else's revolution, are marginalized, defeated and victimized. Resistance or fighting for their own interests is out of the question (the only character to utter that possibility, the Covey in *The Plough and the Stars* is the laughing-stock of the play). An intimation of what could become a real working-class consciousness is the endurance and resilience of the victims and their spirit of solidarity at the end of the same play. In this spirit are also included the protestant woman, Bessie Burgess, and the English soldiers. But one may wonder whether this endurance and this embryonic solidarity goes beyond the mood of tragic resignation which also prevails at the end of Synge's *Riders To the Sea*. If that is correct, if fate provides the last answer, the poor of the Dublin tenements are in virtually the same position as Synge's marginals (incidentally, Fluther and Joxer would not do badly in a Synge play). The other alternative implicitly contained in O'Casey's position - and one that could meet with Yeats's approval, though not with O'Casey's, I think - is that the poor better stick, however grudgingly, to their station in life, hoping for, rather than making a better future. What saves these plays from facile incorporation, however, is that O'Casey's analysis of the place of the Irish working-class in the struggle for Ireland's independence is basically sound. Any further step that includes organized resistance, will have to start from these premisses. It was a step O'Casey was himself to make in *The Silver Tassie* (first produced in London in 1929) and in later plays. But, as Yeats rightly sensed in turning the play down, it placed its author outside the Abbey Theatre formation. "It was time for Sean to go".[61]

Forms

Formational analysis is not the same as historical or literary (formal) analysis, but on account of its intermediary position it allows one to ask questions to both history and the individual work of art. That is its chief interest. We have seen that Yeats's ideological horizon and his critique of the catholic Irish middle-class was nourished and limited by his liberal humanism, tinged with shades of authoritarianism, that Synge speaks from a position of extreme (almost anarchic) individualism and that O'Casey's early plays are imbued with a working-class consciousness that has not yet declared itself. The common ground between these three positions is that the critique of

---

[61] O'Casey, *Autobiographies II*, op.cit., p. 231.

Irish middle-class society it contains, can still be "contained" by that society, since it is made from within or from the edges of that society, not from outside. The need for a serious and organized resistance to that society has not found, nor could it find, a concrete embodiment in these plays. When it is there, as in O'Casey and Synge, and to some extent even in Yeats, it has to remain abstract, it has to project itself into dreams, it becomes an object of the imagination, cut up into many fanciful bits. The rationale behind that projection seems to be that fantasy may serve as an antidote to frustration, poverty and suffering.

From fantasy as an antidote to fantasy as a literary mode is but one step. The work of the Abbey Theatre playwrights discussed here has been widely praised for its high degree of poetic realism, a quality which, as one can see now, is in this case but the literary equivalent, of the historical notions of deadlock and makeshift. Any literary analysis that fails to establish this link is, I think, misconceived (by which I do not mean that the link cannot be established intuitively, as in so much valuable critical work). What the present study hopes to clarify is why certain subjective critical evaluations are good guesses, whereas others are not. Thus it would allow one to see the superiority of studies on Synge that show him, not as a slice of life artist, but as someone who wanted "the impossible seem inevitable";[62] who indulged more in the marvel of a grand story and a fine song than in the condition of the peasant or the labourer in the west of Ireland; who wanted us to listen to the racy and daring speech of his vagrants and tinkers, to enjoy the mixture of the heroic and the ludicrous in his plays along with the humour that makes everything shining; who wanted us above all to see the reversal of values that pervades all his plays. In the same vein my formational analysis would have a marked preference for studies on O'Casey that show him as "a city Synge", with his love of the Bible and Shakespeare, his gift to render the witty, hyperbolic and saucy talk of the Dublin tenements, his versatility in mixing pseudo-learned phrases, eulogy, invective and lyrics, his comic use of melodramatic elements, such as: stock characters, caricature, mock-battles, gag lines, tomfoolery, etc., his violent switches from low comedy to tragedy and back or their juxtaposition (epitomized, for example, by the sound of bullets over the card game in *The Plough and the Stars*) etc. As for Yeats, there is very little danger of not seeing the *poetic* side of his realism. Here it is rather the *realism* itself that is often underrated. Formational analysis may remind one that Yeats was deeply involved in the Irish society of his time, and that it would be extremely unlikely not to find repercussions of that involvement in his plays. What matters, then, is to understand that, through poetic devices like stylization of gesture,

---

62 See T.R.Whitaker (ed.), *Twentieth Century Interpretations of The Playboy of the Western World* (Englewood Cliffs, New Jersey: Prentice-Hall, 1969), p. 13.

voice, costume and décor on the one hand, and of character (masks, types), plot (myths, legends, tales) and theme ("the deep of the mind") on the other, Yeats was always "leaning out to reality", i.e. that he was presenting imagined alternatives to problems of great importance, also for the Ireland of his time: the nature of self-sacrifice, the difficulty of love in a land of hatred, the need for destruction and rebirth, the Nietzschean joy in the face of destruction, the role of the artist in his society, the dialectics of change...

Louis DIELTJENS.

BANVILLE AND BEING:
THE NEWTON LETTER AND HISTORY

It would be difficult to imagine a literature that is so positively obsessed with the national past as the one Ireland has produced in this century. The Irish poets, novelists and dramatists continue to return to the nation's past in order to make sense of the complexities of their existence in the present. Seamus Heaney supplies an etymology of the name of the house in which he was born, in order to comment on the present state of affairs in Ulster and he finds in the Bog People in Jutland metaphors to cope with present sectarian violence. Flann O'Brien's *At Swim-Two-Birds* has Finn McCool and Mad Sweeney in Dublin in the thirties and Brian Friel in *Translations* returns to the nineteenth century. Reasons for this obsession are not too hard to come by, one may simply refer to the essentially historical arguments given by both parties to the Ulster troubles and one must agree with the Irish wit who claimed that Chomsky was wrong about his famous sentence: in Ireland colourless green ideas do sleep furiously.

In the novels of John Banville we can find the same interest in the past, but there is an important difference. Like a number of Irish poets and novelists in the fifties and sixties, he does not seem to be interested in the national past but in a wider European history, more precisely, in Banville's case, in the history of ideas, of science, centred around the lives of Copernicus, Kepler, Newton and Einstein. Of the three novels of this tetralogy that have already been published, *Kepler* and *Doctor Copernicus* come closest to what one can expect of the genre "historical novel"; they describe the lives of the two scientists who were responsible for a revolution in man's image of the cosmos he lives in and of his own place in it. Copernicus's destruction of the Ptolemaic cosmology has always been the supreme example of a scientific revolution and it has played an important role in recent discussions by historians and philosophers of science because it represents a clear change of what Thomas S. Kuhn has called "paradigms". This revolution has also fascinated phenomenological historians such as Hans Blumenberg, who wrote a long study on *Die Genesis der kopernikanischen Welt*. Finally, this revolution in cosmology has been claimed as a paradigm by later iconoclasts: there is Kant who is erroneously believed to have described his accomplishment. in the second preface to the *Kritik der reinen Vernunft* as a "Copernican revolution" and Freud too, at the end of the eighteenth of his

Introductory Lectures on Psychoanalysis, compares his project to that of Copernicus.

One can therefore conclude that Banville's decision to write this tetralogy does not simply represent an arbitrary change of subject-matter or novelistic sub-genre, it should be seen as an ambitious project to investigate the very foundations of the scientific world-view that has shaped the world we live in today. These novels address the assumptions underlying the rationalist world-view and I will attempt to show here how, with *Birchwood,* Banville clears the ground for these epistemological concerns and how, with *The Newton Letter,* he comes to a kind of conclusion. In the process we will also look at Banville's view of history and of the historical novel.

The blurb of the American edition of Banville's second novel shows no doubts about the genre the book belongs to: "This beautifully written Gothic novel is set in the west of Ireland during the time of the Great Famine in the 1850s". The book's dedication "To the Dunham-Shermans, Stepan-Candaus, and the Browns" also points to the fact that we are dealing with a Big House novel, a genre that in the nineteenth century put Ireland on the literary map with novels such as *Castle Rackrent* and *The Real Charlotte. Birchwood* has all the ingredients of this type of novel: the powerful father starts to drink and gamble and manages to lose his estate and the mother is a figure from a Poe story, pale and slowly losing touch with reality. The grandparents are suitably picturesque, the grandfather a doddering eccentric, the grandmother a bossy matriarch who manages to die by spontaneous combustion. The rest of the story has the unruly peasants, rebellious gipsies and other trouble-makers, the breakdown of all order during the great potato famine and the killing of the inhabitants of the Big House during an attack of the insurgents.

The decline and fall of a great family was a popular theme in romantic literature, not just in Ireland, but also in England, continental Europe and even in the United States where E. A. Poe's "The Fall of the House of Usher" is one of its most powerful elaborations. In an increasingly democratic and bourgeois world this type of literature describes the demise of an over-civilised aristocratic class which is not able to put up a defense against the "filthy modern tide". And here we come across a really Irish variant of this romantic *topos,* the retro-active creation of an aristocratic, anti-modernist Ascendancy tradition by William Butler Yeats. Yeats claimed that Ireland had produced a class of strong and independent men who opposed, from the eighteenth century onwards, the empiricism, the science and the parliamentary democracy they associated with England.

Born in such a community, Berkeley with his beliefs in perception, that abstract ideas are mere words, Swift with his love of perfect nature, of the Houyhnhnms, his disbelief in Newton's system and every sort of machine, Goldsmith and his delight in the particulars of common life that shocked his contemporaries, Burke with his conviction that all States not grown like a forest tree are tyrannies, found in England the opposite that stung their own thought into expression and made it lucid.[1]

In his other essays and in his poetry, Yeats propagated this belief in an indigenous protestant tradition he thought just as important to the establishment of an independent state as its Gaelic counterpart. Seamus Deane has challenged this view of Irish history in an article appropriately called "The Literary Myths of the Revival: A Case for their Abandonment". He shows how Yeats's view of the Irish eighteenth and nineteenth centuries is based on a theory of history which bears a close resemblance to other such theories in the Romantic aesthetics of Coleridge, Blake, Carlyle and William Morris and which sees history primarily as the history of the imagination. All of these writers have rendered their aesthetic theories as stories, but Yeats's view of the Ascendancy has been much more influential than other stories, not only in literature, with the Big House novel still alive today, but also in the criticism of Yeats's poetry, of the Irish Revival and of Irish history as such.

The problem is that this view is simply wrong: because, as Deane writes, the Protestants were not really aristocrats and were seen by the native Irish as people of no blood and because they were an essentially bourgeois formation. Deane claims that the results of this mythologising can still be read in Irish literature: "We historicize in order to poeticize, and Ireland, in consequence, begins to cease to be an actuality and begins increasingly to become a metaphor of the self."[2].

Birchwood is clearly an Irish Big House novel: there is a potato famine, the peasants speak a different language, the Lawlesses are not Catholic, there are gombeen men, English soldiers who talk of "Fucking micks", Gabriel's home is close to a city where monks were slaughtered by Cromwell and where Richard FitzGilbert Clare, Earl of Pembroke stood on the ramparts and Gabriel shows himself a worthy member of his class when he observes:

---

[1] W.B.Yeats, "Bishop Berkeley," in *Essays and Introduction* (London: Macmillan, 1971), p. 402.
[2] Seamus Deane, "The Literary Myths of the Revival: A Case for their Abandonment," in *Myth and Reality in Irish Literature*, ed. Joseph Ronsley (Waterloo: Wilfrid Laurier University Press, 1977), p. 323.

> As my people knew, and lucky they did, there is nothing
> that will keep the Irish in their place like a well-appointed
> mansion. They may despise and hate you, only put a fine big
> house with plenty of windows in it up on a hill and bejapers
> you have them be the balls, stunned into cringing, cap-
> touching coma.[3]

But there are also a number of elements in this novel which do not fit into a mid-nineteenth century frame: disregarding for the moment references to the literature and philosophy of the twentieth century, there is the photograph Gabriel carries with him and which depicts his mother as a child, Gabriel's mother wears castoff clothes "straight out of the gay nineties", there are bananas in the house, and a telephone, and the troubles with the tenants could very well refer to the twenties of this century. There are indications that the events described take place in the youth of somebody Banville's age: a hundred years ago there was another potato famine when Gabriel Godkin, our hero's great-great-grandfather arrived and stole the estate from Joseph Lawless.

But Birchwood, its inhabitants, the gipsies and the peasants seem to live in a time-less universe that does not exactly coincide with any one historical period but that shares elements with a number of them. The most strikingly anachronistic aspect in this book is the overwhelming references to literature and philosophy. The book opens with an adaptation of Descartes' *cogito* and ends with the last sentence of Wittgenstein's *Tractatus logico-philosophicus*; in the first chapter there are scores of references to *A la recherche du temps perdu*, later to Yeats and to Joyce, to *Dubliners*, *A Portrait*, *Ulysses* and *Finnegans Wake*, to Shakespeare and Dante, de Sade and Petronius. This intertextuality differs radically from the kind we may find in John Fowles's *The French Lieutenant's Woman* where the object is to render a picture of a woman who is both of her own time and who points ahead to ours and it seems to me closer to what Vladimir Nabokov does in novels such as *Ada*.

Seamus Deane already singled out *Birchwood* as the only modern Big House novel that addresses "wider questions about fiction, its nature and status, its methods and its philosophy which we associate with Borgès, Nabokov, Barth and others" and which belongs to "the Joyce, Flann O'Brien, Beckett experimental tradition" (321). Needless to say, Banville is aware of these experiments; for *Hibernia* he reviewed novels by Nabokov, Barth, John Gardner, Marquez, Fowles, etc.

---

[3] John Banville, *Birchwood* (New York: W.W.Norton, 1973), p. 45.

Banville refers to other works of literature in details, names, plot elements and in short descriptions. The references to Proust in the first chapter all deal with the genre of the memoir: the illusion we have of remembering the past while in reality it can only be brought back in chance sensations, which Gabriel calls "madeleines"; there is a reference to a "lost child, misplaced in time," and the significantly altered title of Proust's novel: "In this search for time misplaced." The other giant of the modernist novel, Joyce, could not be absent in this early work of a young Irish novelist. The narrator's name, Godkin, could be a reference to Stephen's description of the artist as a God; in the first chapter there is a white cloud sailing into a blue bowl of sky, where in the first chapter of *Ulysses* a similar thing happens; the photograph is of a girl who smiles dreamily, "as though she were listening to some mysterious music", like Gretta Conroy in "The Dead," who also married somebody called Gabriel; the day of the narrator's birth there is an apocalyptic moment which resembles the central scene in "Circe" and it is followed by a policemen's skull being split by an ashplant; Gabriel vows to go on his "quest in silence cunningly" like Stephen Dedalus and Michael is Gabriel's "cold mad brother," almost the same words Anna Livia uses to describe her father at the end of *Finnegans Wake*.

As far as I know, Yeats is only referred to once, almost at the end of the book, when Gabriel returns to his home and finds the summerhouse invaded by pigeons, starlings, a hive of bees; just as Yeats does in "Meditations in Time of Civil War," a work that establishes the poet's view of the Protestant Ascendancy and their houses:

> The bees build in the crevices
> Of loosening masonry, and there
> The mother birds bring grubs and flies
> My wall is loosening; honey-bees,
> Come build in the empty house of the stare.[4]

There are also numerous references to the Bible: the twins are called Michael and Gabriel; on p. 11 a confrontation between Granny Godkin and the newly-wed parents of Gabriel turns into a picture of the Holy Family: "The old woman's eyes flickered toward the open door, where Mama hovered, and Joseph turned and stared at his wife with an icy eye. 'Jesus,' he muttered." Shakespeare has supplied a number of characters: the owner of the circus is called Prospero, the process-server is addressed as Malvolio, Silas treats his monkey as a kind of Caliban and he ends his performance with "Gentles, gentles, our revels now are ended" (p.110). In addition, Francis C. Molloy has pointed out that the book's opening mimics that of Dante's *Vita nuova*, but the differences

---

[4] W.B.Yeats, *Collected Poems* (London: Macmillan, 1978), p. 230.

are striking: instead of a rubric "The new life begins," the heading reads, *the beginning of the old life*; Dante intended to gather in his book of memory "the meaning if not the words", Gabriel wants to tell the story, if not the meaning "of the fall and rise of Birchwood, and of the part Sabatier and I played in the last battle". When we come to the end of the book, we will know that this Sabatier is not a person, but a knife which does not really play any role in the last battle. But Sabatier is a partial anagram of Beatrice, the name of the central character in the *Vita nuova* and of the narrator's mother in this novel. The ninth chapter of Book II begins with a familiar sentence: "I was now midway upon my journey, stumbling in darkness" and Gabriel's voyage through a famine-ridden Ireland does indeed read like a season in hell.

Silas, the leader of the gipsies, describes a feast which his good friend Trimalchio laid on for him with the words supplied by Petronius Arbiter and he even curses in Latin on that occasion; one of the women in his band is called Sibyl and Gabriel is often referred to as Caligula or "little boots". The book opens with a poem by Catullus and has Greek mythological echoes, mainly to the Oedipus myth. As in Nabokov's novels (there is an Ada in this book too), these references are not structural, they are just little titbits for the observant reader who recognizes a detail, admires the writer's cleverness and is drawn into his confidence.

Another postmodernist characteristic of this novel is the use of names: we have two archangels and a Holy Family; a servant called Nockter and a peasant called Cotter; the two families are called Lawless and Godkin; there is the Beatrice-Sabatier near-anagram; the circus has a Justin and Juliette and an Ada-Ida twin. As in some of Nabokov's novels, almost everything in this book happens twice: Parts I and II both end in fires; at the end of Part II Magnus is killed when an exploding bullet hits the back of his head, the same thing happens to the last of the Molly Maguires. The picture with which Gabriel opens the book depicts a young girl in a white dress leaning "from the dark into the light smiling blithely, dreamily, ..." When Gabriel sees his brother again after the massacre, it is "a figure in a white gown ... a face leaned out into the sunlight and looked up at me with terrible teeth clenched in a grimace." This doubleness is not surprising in a novel about twins that has mirrors everywhere. From the comparison of memories to the world in the depths of mirrors to the broken mirrors of the destroyed summerhouse where Gabriel finally faces his rival and brother, there are mirrors everywhere. But mirrors can lie too, and their most obvious lie is the confusion between the sexes; Gabriel thinks his twin is a sister, Michael dresses up like a woman when he joins the circus; there are the androgynous twins, the Molly Maguires, etc.

A final characteristic of the postmodernist novel is its self-consciousness, its "narcissicism" to use a term introduced by Linda Hutcheon. This is clear in the structure of the book, a reconstruction of the past by Gabriel who keeps interrupting the narrative to stress his inability to express the things that really happened and to comment on his narrative. This is also obvious in the references to Prospero, the invisible owner of the circus, who seems at some point to be controlling Gabriel's quest like an omniscient narrator or like Clare Quilty, that other androgynous arranger, but who then turns out not to exist, "so I became my own Prospero, and yours." At the end of his story Gabriel writes: "So here then is an ending, of a kind, to my story. It may not have been like that, any of it. I invent, necessarily." The book then ends with "whereof I cannot speak, thereof I must be silent" and it is with this movement from Descartes to Wittgenstein that I return to the theme of history.

Like *The French Lieutenant's Woman, Birchwood* is a post-modernist historical novel, with its self-consciousness of its own fictional character, its fabulation, its anachronistic elements and finally its choice of a model in the literature of the time it describes, Thomas Hardy on the one hand, Maria Edgeworth on the other. But *Birchwood* is much more radical in its skepticism about reconstructing the past: when Fowles's theme, an existentialist modern woman in a Victorian context, is adorned on one level with available historical data --statistics, medical reports, quotations from Marx, Darwin-- *Birchwood* almost completely lacks this realist level: as I have tried to show above, the story is situated in Ireland, but the time is rather difficult to pinpoint; there are too many contradictory hints and the whole novel seems to take place in a mythical never-neverland. *The French Lieutenant's Woman* has as its central image the picture of a woman standing at the end of a deserted quay and staring out to sea.[5] This is an essentially visual perception (Fowles calls it a "still") and when the image was incorporated into the opening of the novel, it is through a telescope that we see Sarah for the first time. *Birchwood* too has such a visual core in the photograph of the girl on the lawn, which, significantly, Gabriel destroys at the opening of the novel: "when I returned the picture had inexplicably altered, and would not fit into the new scheme of things, and I destroyed it". It is here also that the difference in narrative strategies becomes important: Banville's I-narrator is trying to make sense of the past, Fowles's Charles is a victim of forces beyond his control. This explains the references to Proust; like 'Marcel', Gabriel is trying to recapture the past and he can only do that bit by bit: "We imagine that we remember things as they were, while in fact all we

---

5 John Fowles, "Notes on an Unfinished Novel," in *The Novel Today*, ed. Malcolm Bradbury (Manchester: Manchester University Press, 1977), pp. 136-50.

carry into the future are fragments which reconstruct a wholly illusory past". These bits are called "madeleines" and it is these "extra-ordinary moments when the pig finds the truffle embedded in the mud," these epiphanies in Joyce's terminology, that really structure Gabriel's account. They are creative moments; he writes: "Such scenes as this I see, or imagine I see, no difference, through a glass sharply" and he finds it in a gathering of perfect prisms, a cold and complex harmony that Gabriel finds fascinating in Michael's juggling and with which he in his turn seduces Rosie. Again and again these moments are described in light images, "those rare moments when a little light breaks forth, and something is not explained, not forgiven, but merely illuminated," "planes of pale blue glass in space gliding through illusory, gleaming and perfect combinations." What Gabriel and Banville seem to be looking for is a kind of crystalline structure that can give meaning to the randomness of the world. This search for a disembodied truth is a common theme in modern literature, especially in poetry: we find it in Yeats's "The Statues" and *A Vision* and in Thomas Kinsella's poetry, when in "Downstream" for instance, "The slow, down-streaming dead, it seemed, were blended / One with those silver hordes, and briefly shared / Their order, glittering."

The novel does not seem the right medium for these perceptions, which are visual, static and silent. And like this kind of poetry, the theme leads in prose, whether it is Beckett's or Banville's, to silence. If you compare *Doctor Copernicus, Kepler* and *The Newton Letter*, you can see that process at work: the books seem to become shorter as they get closer to an expression of that silence. It is this pure vision of things as they are, exemplified in the structure of the cosmos, that Kepler and Copernicus are looking for: "a precious something of unearthly frailty and splendour"[6] and that the I-narrator in *The Newton Letter* too talks about, again in visual terms: "Her physical presence itself seemed overdone, a clumsy representation of the essential she. That essence was only to be glimpsed obliquely, on the outer edge of vision, an image always there and always fleeting like the afterglow of a bright light on the retina."[7] What Kepler, Copernicus and Newton discover is that science is a fiction, only one way of making sense of things, one world-view, one Wittgensteinian language game among many. This is maybe clearest in *Doctor Copernicus* where the reference to Wallace Stevens and his supreme fictions thematize the problem. That problem lies in language; as a child Copernicus makes a central discovery: "Everything had a name, but although every name was nothing without the thing named, the thing cared nothing for its name, had no need for a name,

---

[6] John Banville, *Kepler* (London: Panther, 1983), p. 3.
[7] John Banville, *The Newton Letter* (London: Panther, 1984), p. 52-3.

and was itself only." At the end of his life he finds: "All theories are but names, but the world itself is a thing." The theme is already there in *Birchwood:* "The words lay dead in ranks, file beside file of slaughtered music," but it is most obviously thematized in *The Newton Letter:* "Sometimes a word, one's own name even, will briefly detach itself from its meaning and become a hole in the mesh of the world." Newton's second letter once more speaks of the inadequacy of any existing language.

It is almost as if *The Newton Letter* is an answer to the questions formulated in *Birchwood*: although it plays in the present time, it deals with a Big House in the South-East owned by a family called Lawless who have a son called Michael and who are slowly losing their estate. Again there are twins, a drunken father, social differences, and an I-narrator who tries to make sense of the recent past. But one thing is different: the narrator is a historian who has stopped his work on a book about Newton and who is writing to the muse of history Clio to explain why.

At the centre of Banville's writing is the thought that history cannot be written, there are stories, different stories, but the essence, what he calls in *Birchwood* with its Kantian name, the thing-in-itself, always escapes. Banville wavers, like Beckett, between Wittgenstein I and Wittgenstein II, between "I can't go on" and "I'll go on." I believe it would be possible to argue that idealist and romantic philosophies have still not come to terms with Kant and have continually attempted to get at the *noumenon*, which is only possible, in Kant's terms again, by an intellectual intuition. In a way Kant stands, like Michael Lawless at the end of *The Newton Letter*, with a flaming sword at the entrance to the paradise of the supernumerical reality the narrator claims he is pregnant with. It is this nostalgia that directly inspired Rilke's Ninth Elegy and the *Sonnets to Orpheus* Banville quotes from, it is the same nostalgia that lies at the basis of Hofmannsthal's *Brief*, and it is powerfully expressed by Saint Paul in his first letter to the Corinthians, misquoted by Gabriel Lawless: "For now we see through a glass, darkly; but then face to face: now I know in part; but then shall I know even as also I am known". It is a basically religious and mystical privilege granted to just a happy few. At the end of *Finnegans Wake* Joyce satirizes such an idea: fallen man sees but a part of the world,

> whereas for numpa one puraduxed seer in seventh degree
> of wisdom of Entis-Onton he savvy inside true inwardness of
> reality, the Ding hvad in idself id est, all objects (...) allside

showed themselves in trues coloribus resplendent with sextuple gloria of light actually retained, untisintus, inside them(*FW* 611).[8]

Banville seems at times to share Heidegger's belief in the ability of art and especially of literature to say things in such a way as to make them *be* more fully than they are in themselves. *Dichten* is *Denken*. This is not only a theme in the romantic and symbolist literature of poets like Novalis, Rilke, Stefan George, Wallace Stevens, Francis Ponge and René Char, it also involves a philosophical problem. Granted that Wittgenstein and philosophers of science such as Thomas Kuhn and Paul Feyerabend are right and that we all have incommensurable points of view, granted that Derrida is right and that there is no meta-text, why would we then assume that in some way literary discourse is privileged, presumably because it speaks the language of things? It is precisely this aesthetic ontology (which seems to be closely allied to a psychological solipsism) that is left unresolved in *Birchwood*: like `Marcel' in *A la recherche du temps perdu*, the narrator creates his own past out of the shiny bits of glass that are all that is left of his childhood. In *The Newton Letter* we have a writer-historian who goes through a crisis similar to the one Newton experienced at the end of his life. Unlike Newton's crisis it is not linguistic in nature, it does not have anything to do with the relationship between words and things. The narrator leaves his cottage and his book on Newton because, like Copernicus and Kepler, he suddenly realizes that he has completely misunderstood the drama happening before his eyes. He is so absorbed by his own reality that he fails to see the world as it is. He keeps discovering that his interpretations are wrong; reality refuses to conform to his language game. And it is here that Joyce proves stronger than Rilke: *The Newton Letter* is a re-writing of "The Dead," in which Gabriel Conroy suddenly realizes that he is not at the centre of the universe and that is a truly Copernican revolution. Kant writes in the introduction to the *Critique of Pure Reason* that Copernicus discovered that he could explain the movement of the stars better when he assumed that they were fixed and that the observer was moving. Similarly, according to Kant, a metaphysician must assume that the perception of reality depends on the a priori structure of our mind. He does not say that we all perceive differently and that there is no ultimate standard to test our perceptions; on the contrary, he is trying to describe a scientific method in which a hypothesis can be put forward and then tested.

Gabriel Conroy and the narrator of *The Newton Letter* discover that they are only one of the many planets circling the sun. They find, like Newton in the motto of Banville's novel, that they have been "playing on the seashore (...) finding a smoother pebble or a prettier

---

8 James Joyce, *Finnegans Wake* (London: Faber, 1976), p. 611.

shell than ordinary, whilst the great ocean of truth lay all undiscovered" before them. This ocean does not contain the music of the spheres nor the "supernumerous" existence Rilke writes about in the Ninth Elegy, it is the existence of other people, the past and present suffering of others that breaks through the narrator's solipsism and it is that, in the final analysis, that makes this and all kinds of literature relevant.

Geert Lernout

DESMOND HOGAN AND IRELAND'S
POSTMODERN PAST

> So I began to demand of history an Explanation. Only to uncover in this dedicated search more mysteries, more fantasticalities, more wonders and grounds for astonishment than I started with, only to conclude forty years later - notwithstanding a devotion to the usefulness, to the educative power of my chosen discipline - that history is a yarn. And can I deny that what I wanted all along was not some golden nugget that history would at last yield up, but History itself, the Grand Narrative, the filler of vacuums, the dispeller of fears of the dark?
>
> Graham Swift, *Waterland*

Of the newer wave of "British" (i.e. writing in English and published in England) authors that have gained prominence since the late seventies, e.g. Salman Rushdie, Martin Amis, John Banville, Graham Swift, A.N. Wilson, and William Boyd, Desmond Hogan's voice, to my mind, is one of the most distinctive. To date, this younger Irish author (County Galway, 1952), has published three novels, viz. *The Ikon Maker* (1976), *The Leaves on Grey* (1978), and *A Curious Street* (1984), and two volumes of stories, viz. *The Diamonds at the Bottom of the Sea and Other Stories* (1979), and *Children of Lir* (1981), both collected in *Stories* (1982). In all of Hogan's work the history of his native country plays a prominent part. In jagged fragments it intrudes upon these narratives, sometimes shaping the lives of their characters, but more often as rhetorical surplus. As ornamental interludes, setting a tone, an atmosphere; explaining moods, events, actions by implication, by homology, rather than by direct link, involvements of cause and effect. Hogans's most recent novel to date, *A Curious Street*, best illustrates his continuing fascination with Irish history. At the same time, though, it is also a meditation upon that fascination, and upon its relationship to his own writing and contemporary Irish writing in general.

A Curious Street is, at one and the same time, an historical novel, and a novel of education. First and foremost, it is the story of the growth to young manhood of Jeremy Hitchens, the narrator of the book. At the moment of telling his story Jeremy is a sergeant ·in the British Army, stationed in Belfast in the late seventies. It is in order to understand how he got to be where and what he is that Jeremy writes *A Curious Street*. This however, we only find out well into the book; indeed at the very end of its first major part, entitled "childhood."

During this entire first part of *A Curious Street* we are offered, in consecutive fragments, scenes from the life of Alan Mulvanney, an Athlone schoolteacher found shot to death beside the Shannon in 1977, from an unpublished novel called *A Cavalier Against Time* which Alan wrote in the forties, and from the early years of Jeremy Hitchens himself. In a "prologue" we had already been introduced to Alan as a man Jeremy's mother once knew. From "childhood" it appears that Jeremy's mother was rejected as a lover by Alan, who was a (reluctant) homosexual. She fled to England, where she became a whore, and later married a North of England ex-military man, more than twenty years her senior. To her son, though, she keeps on talking about Alan Mulvanney, and about his novel, *A Cavalier Against Time*. When she finally persuades her husband to move his family to Ireland, to her own native town, these tales have become fully as much a part of the boy's memories as the events of his own life. When he starts to imaginatively account for his own childhood, then, he finds he also has to tell about Alan and his novel, and in this way to account for his Irish heritage.

Much the same thing happens in part two of *A Curious Street*, entitled "adolescence". This part is set in the early sixties, the period Jeremy himself lives in his mother's West of Ireland town. Just as for the time of his childhood he feels he also has to account for the "Shadows" he inherits from his mother, and through her from one of these shadows, Alan Mulvanney, he how finds he has to account for the lives of the people he gets involved with during his stay in Ireland. However, we find that as he is *writing* of telling the stories of these lives concurrently with that of Alan and his fictional heroes, a peculiar case of contamination takes place, abetted by the uniform narrative rhetoric in which all these stories are swathed.

We find that the story of Lorcan O'Mahony and Eleanor Laffan, the hero and heroine of *A Cavalier Against Time*, sets the pattern for the stories of all other couples in the book. The only development, as time goes by, is that the pattern is enacted in an ever more sordid way as we approach the present. Jeremy's own courtships and his brief marriage form the culmination of a long decline. All relationships in *A Curious Street* move from momentary union, over gradual disillusionment and despair, to a final parting. Especially for the women these experiences are often preceded by genuine loves, which, however, are brief and tragically unfulfilled. Both the defeat of these brief but genuine loves, and the disintegration of the longer relationships of the couples described, are due to divisions between the partners brought about by Irish history.

These divisions are of various kinds: Celt vs. Saxon or Norman, Irish vs. English, Catholic vs. Protestant, tinkers vs. settled inhabitants, West of Ireland vs. East of Ireland Irish. Most of these internal divisions are the result of the English invasions of Ireland, and particularly of Cromwell's decree, in 1653, for the native Irish to find themselves West of the Shannon before the coming spring. In his own person Jeremy Hitchens, the son of an Irish woman and an Englishman, born in England but partly raised in Ireland, and finally a British soldier in Northern Ireland, embodies many of these divisions. In Alan Mulvanney, and in his own Irish boyhood friend Eugene McDermott, Jeremy meets with two characters that offer suggestions as to how imaginatively to deal with these divisions.

Both Alan and Eugene are examples of other-ness in their own society: Alan is homosexual, and Eugene (although he is never openly referred to as such) is often hinted to be so. For both of them this other-ness is a function of their country's history. For both of them, too, it is their country's history that drives them to authorship. As so often in Hogan's fictional universe, homosexuality and creativeness are linked to function as signs of the sensitive Irishman's "discontent" or "unease" with his culture (e.g. *The Ikon Maker* and a number of the stories). For both Alan and Eugene literature provides a solution to this discontent. Alan uses it to try and reunite himself with his country and culture by exploring its past. Eugene resolutely opts for exile from his country and its history and literature.

Alan is obsessed with Irish history, and especially with the coming of the Cromwellians to Ireland. Born in 1919 in Athlone, the town on the Shannon where the native Irish had to cross the bridge going West, he is only too acutely aware of the divisions marking Ireland. Yet, he tries to imaginatively exorcize them: his novel, *A Cavalier Against Time*, has his hero and heroine preaching peace around Ireland in the period immediately preceding the coming of Cromwell. It is an attempt to overcome those divisions that with the coming of Cromwell will become unbreachable. In a sense, Eleanor and Lorcan are waging a battle that, in retrospect, we know to have been lost from the start. Alan admits as much by having his characters go into exile, Eleanor marrying a wealthy merchant in Antwerp, Lorcan making his way to the South of Spain and marrying a Moorish girl. He also admits as much by leaving his novel unpublished. This sign of impotence in the literary realm is complemented by his sexual impotence in his affair with Eileen Carmody, later Jeremy Hitchens' mother.

Alan's prospective solution, then, flatly goes against the evidence of his own life. As the stories of the Irish townfolk in *A Curious Street* demonstrate, it also goes against the evidence of the lives of Alan's generation, as well as against that of Jeremy's. Alan, therefore, stands as a negative example to Jeremy. Via his mother, and via his own literary ambitions, Jeremy recognizes himself in Alan. Yet, he realizes that Alan's attempt to lay the divisions of the present by the ghosts of the past is doomed to fail.

The solution offered by Eugene McDermott, Jeremy's bosom friend during his years in Ireland, is exactly the opposite from that offered by Alan Mulvanney. From early life on, Eugene shows a penchant for literature. He stages little dramas with his friends. He is a.voracious reader. However, his preference is for foreign literature (specifically: Russian) rather than Irish. In his own personal past and present no less divided than Alan, he opts for escape rather than for trying to recapture the wholeness of Ireland's past. This attitude is captured in a poem he writes for Jeremy Hitchens, when the latter leaves Ireland. It is a poem of exile, in which figure the words: "a curious street unfolds - pictures." This, of course, is the phrase that Jeremy will borrow for the title of his own novel.

Yet, *A Curious Street* is not a novel of unconditional exile. In fact, like *A Cavalier Against Time*, it deals very much with Ireland, and Irish history. However, it does not do so in the manner of Alan's novel. Jeremy's novel exists precisely by grace of the tension between Alan's and Eugene's ideas on how to imaginatively deal with Ireland, on how to deal with the past from the dividedness of the present. The solution Jeremy hits upon, and which he implements in *A Curious Street,* is to present Irish history not as a tapestry stretching over the centuries, but as "a curious street," a series of separate "pictures". Irish history not as a continuum of facts, events, and ideas, but as a series of sharp discontinuities. These discontinuities are framed by one narrative structure, and are coached in a uniform style. However, structure and style do not serve to veil the discontinuities. Rather, by way of the overt narrative contamination between the lives of its characters, and by its self-revelatory use of narrative voice, *A Curious Street* self-consciously reveals its own rhetorical unifying function, pre-empting it by foregrounding it, and thus actually re-inforcing rather than masking the awareness of discontinuities in its readers. *A Curious Street* is a novel of exile *from within*: it explodes the very myths, the received ideas, the popular and canonized "truths" of Irish history it is appealing to.

In his own novel, then, Jeremy fuses the literary recipes of Alan and Eugene. He self-consciously indicates as much when, on the last page of his novel, he has Alan and Eugene imaginatively also fuse bodily. On that last page too he indicates that both these characters, in the guise in which he portrayed then, have been fictional projections throughout, however "real" they at the same time may have been on his own - as a character, and therefore necessarily also fictional - level. In the last two (shorter) parts of *A Curious Street,* respectively entitled "Aftermath", and "Epilogue". Jeremy himself is shifted into the position of fictional projection. In "Aftermath" this is done by speaking of Jeremy, in a couple of sections, in the third person singular. In "Epilogue" a new character is introduced, that sometimes speaks of himself in the third person, but ends up the novel in the first person singular. This new character, both as to appearance and to personal past, is a very close replica indeed of Hogan himself. Hence, if *A Curious Street*, as told by its first person narrator Jeremy Hitchens, is the fictional story of its own genesis, it at the same time self-consciously reveals itself as such also on the level of reality. Jeremy Hitchens' programme for writing about being an Irishman in this last quarter of the twentieth century, then, likewise seems to be that of Desmond Hogan.

As the embodiment of this programme, *A Curious Street* then becomes both a reflection upon earlier uses of history in Irish literature, and an instance of Postmodernism. The solution that Alan Mulvanney adopts to overcome the divisions he feels internally rending him, and his country, apart is typical of the use Irish literature has been put to in the service of the Irish struggle against the English. At the same time, it is a solution typical of literary Modernism. The Modernists saw a similar kind of division as that felt by Alan to be characteristic for his country as endemic - albeit for different reasons - to all of Western culture in the early part of the twentieth century. For them this division manifested itself in a dissolution of what Jean François Lyotard, in his book *La condition postmoderne* (1979), termed "metanarratives" (in the translation of Hassan and.Hassan 1983): those beliefs justifying Western (bourgeois) society to itself since - roughly - the Renaissance. As examples of these metanarratives we can mention economics, religion, history etc.: the systems of rules by which the operations of the world, of society, culture, and man could be explained. By the end of the nineteenth century, many of these metanarratives had come to be doubted. For the Modernists, the First World War gave them the final blow: they saw their world as irreparably torn apart.

Even if the Modernists used their own works to express the fragmentation of their world, they at the same time lamented it.

Therefore they appealed to the authority of those metanarratives they saw as lost to provide unity to their works: Eliot's myths, Pound's use of history, Faulkner's use of Southern history and mythology. In this way art, literature, projected a remedy to fragmentation and came to function, in the absence of all other sources of genuine authority, as itself the final metanarrative. In view of their particular circumstances, then, it was only natural that (a number of) Irish Modernists appealed to history as the unifying metanarrative in their works.

Jeremy's, and Hogan's, self-conscious use of Irish history in *A Curious Street,* however, posits Irish history not as a "true" legitimation for refound unity and wholeness, but as a verbal construct projected upon the Irish past. It is this linguisticity, and its self-conscious revelation, that stand at the heart of the postmodern way of writing. As I have tried to argue elsewhere, postmodernism to this end turns fictional (sub)genres against themselves, as Hogan here does with the historical novel, which is conventionally used to underline myths of nationhood, of national grandeur, etc. (cfr. Conscience's *De Leeuw van Vlaanderen*). Hogan uses the conventions of the genre precisely to destroy these notions.

With *A Curious Street* Hogan destroys the idea, typical for a previous generation of Modernist Irish writers, that literature is in itself a useful means for the creation of national unity. As the epigraph to this paper, from Graham Swift's *Waterland* (1983), may show, similar concerns with regard to the uses history and literature may be put to are shared by other writers of Hogan's generation. Together with other younger Irish writers such as John Banville, then, whose novels take a similarly "linguistic" view of history, and of literature itself, Hogan claims for Irish fiction a place as prominent in Postmodernism as it used to hold in Modernism.

Theo D'Haen

BRIAN FRIEL'S DRAMA AND THE LIMITS OF LANGUAGE

Brian Friel, a Northern Irish playwright born in County Tyrone in 1929, is one of the leading dramatists in Ireland today.Together with the actor Stephen Rea he formed the Field Day Theatre Company in 1980, a project which can best be described as a revival of the role the Abbey played at the beginning of the century.Like Yeats, the members of Field Day, all of them from Northern Ireland, believe that the social and political revolution in their country should be led by an imaginative consciousness. In other words, they believe that no cultural initiative in Ireland can be dissociated from the political dialogue, but, on the contrary, should result in a renewed definition of a dying nation. The political idealism of the company is particularly concentrated on language: according to them, language is the prime redeemer of reality, the most important element in the restoration of the island's unity.Furthermore, their artistic creations appear to be questioning the value of age-old truths concerning the "Irish identity" and all it stands for. As Seamus Deane puts it convincingly at the end of his pamphlet:

> The oppressiveness of the tradition we inherit has its source in our own readiness to accept the mystique of Irishness as an inalienable feature of our writing and, indeed, of much else in our culture [...] the myth of Irishness, the notion of Irish unreality, the notions surrounding Irish eloquence [...]
> Everything [...] has to be rewritten - i.e. re-read .[1]

In what follows I intend to prove that underneath the apparently colourful speeches of Friel's characters the dramatist voices an incisive scepticism about the possibilities of the linguistic medium. Too often the author has been praised for his fluent colloquialism according to the verbal tradition of Irish theatre. Critics fail to pay attention to the frequent hesitations and stammerings of the speaker and to Friel's concern with language as cover, distortion, mental colonialism and so forth.

Throughout his drama the playwright seems to be interrogating people's excessive use of discourse: his characters indulge in meaningless babble which isolates them from true communication; they

---

[1] Seamus Deane, "Heroic Styles: the Tradition of an Idea", *A Field Day Pamphlet*, no. 4, 1984, 17-8.

hide themselves behind verbal smokescreens; or they exploit language for their own purposes.Closely connected to this language problem is the omnipresent unease with roles and conventions: protagonists repeat each other's lines, refuse to obey the stage-directions (*Living Quarters* (1978), *The Loves of Cass McGuire* (1966)) and even interchange identities (*The Communication Cord*) (1983)). Indeed, it can be argued that the recurrent impotence of the personae to play their own parts is indicative of the artist's underlying distrust of stereotyped posturing. In this line of thinking, the plays under discussion can be read as a plea for the re-examination of Ireland's political and cultural identity. Accordingly, Friel's art becomes a significant contribution towards the liquidation of all sterile traditions. It will be my argument that his dramatic art is an attempt to transcend the trappings of a civilization as it has arisen from centuries of oppression. Or more explicitly, his dilemma is that of the modern Anglo-Irish playwright doubting his nation's love of "fine words" in a dramatic style that continues the Abbey-tradition.

Of Friel's earlier plays, *Philadelphia, Here I Come* (1965) most clearly deals with the social implications of the crisis of the word. As a matter of fact, the greater part of the early works (up to 1970) is ostensibly concerned with the tragic failure of the individual to reveal his deeper emotions. In these dramas (as in *Cass McGuire* or *Lovers* (1968)) the dramatist concentrates on the gap between private consciousness on the one hand and the oppressive forces of the outside world on the other. As a result, the characters see themselves driven back into social protocols that smother the development of the ego.

Philadelphia is about a young Irishman whose private and public lives have been a failure because of the stagnant conditions of Irish small-town existence. At the onset of the play he is contemplating emigration to America "ecstatic with joy and excitement"; but soon we learn that his "eejiting about" is no more than a rhetorical guard against painful memories and the innermost call for affection haunting him in the persona of Private Gar. The protagonist has been imitating and clowning for so long that it has become impossible to admit to himself the realities of his life, or to express what he truly feels.

Ballybeg, a fictive village in County Donegal, represents the old rural society, notoriously characterized by deadening conventions and emotional shallowness. As in Joyce's *Portrait*, any individual who tries to live beyond its traditions is doomed to oppressive anxiety, alienation and feelings of guilt. People here withdraw into hypocritical behaviour and buffoonery because they have never learned how to establish communal relationships of any kind. Gar's agony, then, is the frustration of a young man gifted with picturesque humorous speech, but unable to ventilate his grievances and legitimise his decision to leave. Indeed, Private's continuous flow of talk sharply contrasts with the stammerings and hesitations of his double (i.e. when he cannot keep up his public image of the mountebank). Ironically, however, his eloquent deliveries can be heard only by the latter so that the youth finds himself reduced to the same verbal isolation as his taciturn father.

All the characters in this play aspire for some vital response from those around them - think of Gar's desperate cry for meaningful contact on p.51: "Just - just let me talk a bit more -let me communicate with someone [...]".[2] But any inclination towards sympathy is stifled by the very milieu in which it should have its fullest consummation: Lizzy is unable to enunciate her anguished desire for a son; "the boys" all overact because they feel they should disguise their grief at Gar's departure; and the silent S.P. is too remote to articulate his worry about the boy's emigration. By demonstrating how endless talk can alienate the speaker from himself and others, *Philadelphia* appears to be questioning the emphasis on elocution that characterizes Irish theatre.

Ultimately the artist's scepticism concerning exaggerated posturing and the uncomplicated use of the verbal medium touches upon the oppression of tradition in Ireland. His is the voice of the colonized writer expressing himself in a language not his own. To quote Friel himself:

> We flirt with the English language, but we haven't absorbed it [...]
> It's accepted outside the island, you see, as "our great facility with
> the English language" [...] that's all oul [sic] rubbish. A language is
> much more profound than that. It's not something we produce for
> the entertainment of outsiders. And that's how Irish theatre is
> viewed indeed, isn't it?[3]

In succeeding plays - *The Freedom of the City* (1974), *Quarters, Volunteers* (1979) - the artist focuses his attention on the erosion of Irish society and the important function language plays in this crisis. Human speech is shown to serve as a vehicle of corruption in the political and cultural chaos characterizing Ireland. *Freedom*, more particularly, concentrates on the hypocrisy involved in official reports. Language here is exposed as a means of manipulation in the hands of the news media, the clergy, science, the law and any political movement. All of these exploit the "seizure" of the Guildhall to bring home their prejudices on the civil rights march. In a sense, the story contains two

---

[2] Brian Friel, *Selected Plays* (London, Boston: Faber, 1984).
[3] Fintan O'Toole, "The Man from God Knows Where. An Interview with Brian Friel", *In Dublin*, No. 165, October 1982, 20-3, 21.

major plot lines: the Guildhall events enacted on stage and the facts as the reconstruction pronounces on them. The development of these contrastive threads, then, shows the discrepancy between the actions as they took place on the one hand and the conclusions reached by the investigators on the other. As in *Faith Healer* (1980), the dramatist probes into the limits of language, that is, into the truth of what is said; accordingly, one could argue that *Freedom* echoes simultaneously the Kantian notion of subjectivity within the individual's perception and the Beckettian suspicions of the representational value of language.

Speech in the play is desecrated as a distortion of reality: a lie in the mouth of the oppressor, an illusion in that of the victim. The voice of reason is set against the voice of imagination and both are found inadequate. Equally, Friel seems to be making the point that the deepest energies of the Irish soul have always been expressed in words, but that this is a fact fraught with danger: it inevitably leads to tendentious interpretation of history and the creation of false mythologies. The dramatist dismisses as dishonest all official language: the frozen generalities of the sociologist, the pseudo-objectivity of the judge, the nationalist idiom of sacrificial martyrdom and the imaginative language of the race (embodied by Lily and Skinner).

Freedom is an amalgam of repetitions, ambiguities, clichés, pauses, mispronunciations, instances of amnesia ... The recurrent periods of silence in this tragi-comedy, therefore, get specific significance: it is the artist's attempt to redeem the phrase out of the "market place" into genuine reticence. The total collapse of discourse - intolerable for the speaker - becomes a necessity if all old priorities are to be annihilated. The silence that remains is the space where real thinking can take place and new values are created. In particular, it permits Lily to go beyond the limit of what the ideals of eloquence allow her to say:

> And in the silence before my body disintegrated in a purple convulsion, I thought I glimpsed a tiny truth: that life had eluded me because never once in my forty-three years had an experience, an event, even a small unimportant happening been isolated, and assessed, and articulated[4]

Her moment of insight sharply contrasts with Skinner's final withdrawal into extreme self-delusion. His decision to die in "defensive flippancy" can be interpreted either as a desperate justification of a life-time of joking, or as the youth's actual identification with the myth of the roguish Irishman. In either case, Friel accuses the officials of taking him seriously in his role of harlequin, i.e. of killing him for acting the

---

[4] *Selected Plays*, p.150.

mountebank they have made of him. Finally, since the judge's use of language cannot describe the state of affairs truthfully, his terminal speech ends in a climactic scene of non-verbal showing. Only the noise of "a fifteen-second burst of automatic fire"[5] is capable of authentic expression.

Quarters is a tragedy about what should or should not have been said at a particular time in the history of a family; about the impossibility to retrieve lost opportunities and the human need to escape from reality. But more importantly, it is the dramatist's major contribution to post-modernist art proclaiming its own extinction. Friel's competent piece of work questions itself in its several dimensions: as written by the artist, enacted by the players and perceived by the audience. Whereas *Freedom* mainly exposed the falsity of public reports, this work has as its theme the inauthenticity of its artistic medium (echoing Nietzsche's recognition that man's genius is one of lies). The work primarily deals with a character called Sir, who has summoned all the members of the Butler family in order to re-enact the celebration of the father's return from the Middle East. However, this reiteration soon turns out to be exquisitely painful for the relatives. In the scenes outside the play-within-play they frequently disagree over the way Sir's ledger deals with certain events (Helen in *Selected Plays*, p.188: "It's not right [...] It's distorted - inaccurate."). The players' unease with the text is further reflected by their attempt to alter the sequence of the facts and by their formal protest against the definition of the parts to be played. It is obvious that the failure of the script to capture the happenings of that day is related to the problems involved in the resurrection of a verbal construct of the past. Any recollection of discourse necessarily implies subjective reading, translation and interpretation of the written material and eventually leads to an arbitrary recreation.

Again Friel's mistrust of language as perversion of reality cannot be dissociated from his distaste for stereotypes (roles) as violation of the self. Furthermore, the play explicitly suggests that the writer's creation of himself (through his art) threatens to turn into an act of self-destruction at the very moment his characters become so ontologically real that he loses all control over them.[6] In *Quarters* the dramatis personae refuse to play certain scenes, take some liberties in their acting or repeat each other's words. The actors' theatrical opposition to their roles embodies, in fact, the individual's existential struggle with a medium that hampers self-expression. Their refusal to play is man's futile search for communication through the unspoken. But since life is

---

5 *Selected Plays*, p. 169.
6 cf. Flann O'Brien's *At Swim-Two-Birds*, in which the unnamed narrator tells the story of the novelist Trellis, whose characters develop a personality of their own and for this purpose drug their creator.

a process of self-creation, and silence forces us into non-being, the players reluctantly go on the stage (thereby saving themselves and Friel from extinction).

Faith Healer is undoubtedly Friel's most scrutinizing examination into the power of the writer. Its content (the story about Francis Hardy's artistic performances) and form (the four monologues) are made to converge into a harmonious reflection on the art of story-telling.[7] Frank Hardy is a portrait of the artist as "showman", as dramatist totally absorbed by his professional enterprise to the point of becoming his own God. More ruthlessly than ever Friel explores the world of language which he inhabits: he shows how its mysterious force can become fortune or fate, creative or destructive. As in *Freedom* and *Quarters*, the protagonists' reconstruction of events turns out a misrepresentation due to the process of selection, emphasis and interpretation. Again we find art or language thinking about themselves as modification of thoughts, feelings and situations. The play demonstrates how any verbal expression claiming truth evolves into an act of imperialism. More specifically, Friel shows up the speaker's underlying faith that he can alter circumstances through imaginative force. This axiom is worked out in the story of the faith healer, who - like Christy Mahon in Synge's *Playboy* - transforms his world by the power of imagination. Frank introduces himself as "the Fantastic Francis Hardy, Faith Healer"[8], possessing "A craft without an apprenticeship, a ministry without responsibility, a vocation without a ministry"[9].

His skill resides in the creative strength of his fantasy, allowing him to evoke as real any imagined situation - an example of the Sartrean approach to language as appropriation. The same idea also lies behind the characters' reformulation of the past in accordance with their self-image. In Sartre's philosophy all authors primarily regard the word as a way of creating or possessing the thing. They believe they can introduce into the sentence the object described. Because of this magical notion of the phrase, one's writing is always a non-communicative showing off (a writing for its own sake). Frank's healing art too is one of complete mastery over the world: he recreates it "according to some private standard of excellence of his own"[10], or people are totally obliterated "allowed to dissolve and vanish"[11]. His

---

[7] A similar idea is worked out in Richard Kearney's excellent article on "Language: Brian Friel and Ireland's Verbal Theatre" in *Studies. An Irish Quarterly Review*, 72, Spring 1983, 20-56.
[8] *Selected Plays*, p. 332.
[9] *Selected Plays*, p. 333.
[10] *Selected Plays*, p. 346.
[11] *Selected Plays*, p. 345.

talent is the power of illusion, of turning into reality what previously existed only as thought (identical to language in Sartre's view); it is the magic of the word. Accordingly, there is in this play a continuous connection between *what* is remembered and *the way* it is reconstructed, so that the monologues become a re-enactment of the faith healing.

The story is told by three narrators delivering different versions of the events in a Beckettian scene of the isolated speaking mouth; it is Friel's lonely fantasizing by means of the non-stop sound; thus he exploits to the full the listener's dependence on the voice to shape the dramatic vision through the tales it tells. The playwright does not put *the* mirror up to nature, but several mirrors in a multidimensional structure that defies ultimate interpretation. The technique resembles the sonata form, where the themes of the exposition (Frank's first soliloquy) are constantly repeated and reworked into new combinations and sequences (Grace's and Teddy's parts). Each protagonist looks at the past from a different angle and construes a retrospection totally divergent from that of the two others. Things are added, left out, transformed, misinterpreted ... They are made to fit the needs of the characters involved, just like the faith healer invented (cured) or erased people as his ego commanded. Consider, in this respect, the stories relating to the choice of the atmospheric background music: as far as Frank is concerned, the song is Teddy's choice; Grace recalls Frank's insistence on it, and Teddy claims that Gracie picked the song "Because that was the big hit the year she and Frank was married"[12].

To Friel and the speakers equally language is a mode of being. It allows them to project images of themselves in front of an audience that - through its very act of perception - confirms their existence. Indeed, their concern with words is more than a verbal game: this can be inferred from Frank's introduction of himself by way of the banner behind him, or from the episode about the newspaper clipping in part four: "Never knew why I kept it for so long [...] maybe just as an identification"[13]. Gracie, too, needs the verbal explication of things as an affirmation of their validity - "And then because I said it and the doctor wrote it down, I knew it was true ..."[14]. This dependence on linguistic representation is, however, disturbed by the impending dissolution of their monologues implicit in their struggle to find the right word; e.g. Gracie's description of her husband's state of mind before every performance:

---

[12] *Selected Plays*, p. 354.
[13] *Selected Plays*, p. 371.
[14] *Selected Plays*, p.346.

> [...] and he's squatting on the floor of the van - no, not squatting - crouched [...] and happy - no, not happy [...] in complete mastery - yes, that's close to it [...][15].

More distinctively than in any of the other plays, the author dramatizes the individual's struggle to realize himself - Frank as faith healer, Grace as Frank's legal wife and Teddy as professional companion. However, none of them can finally preserve an appropriate selfhood. What is more, Hardy's genuine homecoming has to be paid for with his own death (cf. the protagonists in the *Deirdre*-legend). Friel's suspicions, then, of Frank's - and by extension his own - craft are ultimately indicative of a more inclusive dissatisfaction: notably, with traditional Irish mythology, which he sees as highly in need of renovation if it is to be saved from inanity. As a modern-day version of *Deirdre*, *Faith Healer* both asserts the author's right to alter the ancient plot, but also the mythical plot's final right to appropriate writer and character. It is this unorthodox attitude that also underlies Synge's unique interpretation of the folk-legend through his use of realistic motives and his psychological complexity; Deirdre's narcissism and her romantic fascination with her own legend seem to be echoed by Frank's artistic self-absorption and his final self-destruction.

Let us finally have a closer look at *Translations* (1981), which can be considered as the response to Ireland's language problem by a writer who feels alienated from his culture as a result of centuries of colonization. Friel explores the consequences for a community when its native linguistic landscape is transcribed into a foreign one. At the same time, however, he recognizes the necessity of accepting the facts of history and change, and of renewing one's own culture accordingly.

It is a political play about Ireland's relationship with England and the problems involved in the translation of Irish into English. To argue his point, the playwright has reworked in his dramatic text several paragraphs from Steiner's *After Babel. Aspects of Language and Translation*.[16] In this study George Steiner reflects on the literary act of translating and on language in general, and concludes that in certain civilizations grammar and vocabulary have become a barrier to new feeling. Hence any attempt at truthful communication is bound to fail. Moreover, since any semantic form is embedded in time, the use of a certain idiom (be it a national or individual one) always implies one particular, historically determined world view; Therefore any model of translation is a priori impossible; in Steiner's words: "Time, distance,

---

15 *Selected Plays*, p. 343.

16 For a more detailed discussion of Friel's usage of *After Babel*, see Richard Kearney.

disparities in outlook or assumed reference, make this act more or less difficult"[17].

Friel takes us back to the years just before the Great Famine (1833): that is, when the Irish language was threatened with oblivion by the arrival of a group of English soldiers in charge of the Ordnance Survey Map. Baile Beag is a backward place, whose people live mostly in the past or in the world of ancient myths in order to rise above the present drabness. The locals are interested in the origins of the Gaelic tongue - consider their obsession with Latin and Greek - and in the power of language to confer identity. These concerns are already hinted at in the opening episode: the reader discovers Manus teaching Sarah how to pronounce her name, while Jimmy is "flirting" with Pallas Athena. Hugh, we are told, has gone off to a christening of an illegitimate baby whose name is to reveal the identity of the father. Unfortunately, this culturally secluded community finds itself suddenly invaded by the English oppressor changing the native place names for an Anglicized equivalent. As Owen puts it: their job is "to translate the quaint, archaic tongue you people persist in speaking into the King's good English"[18].

Owen is Hugh's emancipated son, coming back to his birthplace as an interpreter working for the English. He is the typical bilingual exile torn between his conservative family and the progressive "other world". Yolland is his counterpart and Friel's contribution towards the elimination of stereotyped national identities. An English officer "by accident", he is, unlike Captain Lancey, aware of the dangers involved in what he is doing. Moreover, the Lieutenant possesses all the characteristics of the romantic Irishman and feels at home among the local farmers. Nevertheless he realizes he can never be one of them, as every tribal idiom has its own "hermetic core", i.e. a specific historical landscape.

It leaves no doubt that Friel deplores the eradication of the Irish language. He is asking himself the question: what is to become of a people deprived of its native tongue? But he is not a despairing writer. Instead he recognizes that for a modern Irish artist his relation to the past is only part of the story. Besides that there is the more fundamental link with the future, with other cultures and the *present* self. A nation must never cease re-inventing itself "because once we do, we fossilize" Hugh tells us. His defence of his country's need to renew

---

17 George Steiner, *After Babel. Aspects of Language and Translation* (London, New York, Toronto: Oxford University Press, 1975), p. 46.
18 *Selected Plays*, p. 404.

its vernacular gradually develops into a pleading for the revision of history and mythology:

> I look at James and three thoughts occur to me: A - that it is not the literal past, the "facts" of history, that shape us, but images of the past embodied in language [...] B - we must never cease renewing those images; [...] To remember everything is a form of madness.[19]

In other words, if history is to be usable for the present and the future, we must adapt our conception (language) of past events to the stream of life. Exactly because of the continuous flux of happenings definitive statements are impossible but, on the contrary, in constant need of reconstruction. Friel separates himself from the ideological recourse to the idiom of the tribe by exposing the shallowness and exhaustion of the mother-tongue. As the hedge-schoolmaster sees it:

> Yes, it is a rich language, Lieutenant, full of the mythologies of fantasy and hope and self-deception - a syntax opulent with tomorrows. It is our response to mud cabins and a diet of potatoes.[20]

Human speech in this drama functions as a barrier rather than as a means of communication: not only between conflicting cultural identities, but also between people from the same tribe, as evidenced by Jimmy's pitiful cry for companionship in the final scene. Like their fictional predecessors, people in this work cannot articulate their feelings and have to rely on body-language if they want to reach some level of contact: Sarah for instance, can only make herself understood to Manus by means of gestures and facial mimicry. Similarly, all of Maire's and Yolland's attempts to talk to each other result in misunderstanding and only when they avail of non-linguistic expression (or the mere listing of Gaelic place-names) can they convey their love.

Translations successfully transcends the standard opposition between "Irishness" and "Englishness" through its radical dismissal of stereotypes (e.g. Yolland) and ancient values: since Irish has ceased to "match the landscape of fact"[21], the local people have to fall back on Latin and Greek; furthermore, meaningful contact between two hostile nations proves to be possible outside language (Maire and Yolland); even so, English can be poetical (think of Maire's citing of English place

---

[19] *Selected Plays*, p. 445.
[20] *Selected Plays*, p. 418.
[21] *Selected Plays*, p. 419.

names) or ultimately lose its practical use[22]. Contrary to the Republican ideology of martyrdom, the victim in the end is an Englishman (the actual eviction of the inhabitants does not take place in the story).

There is a way, then, in which Yolland's fate resembles that of Skinner (*Freedom*) in that both seem to be punished for adapting the role of stage-Irishman in front of the oppressor. For these reasons it is right to say that more urgently than ever the dramatist appeals for a newly created selfhood in Ireland. If the country is to achieve a genuine cultural and political "homecoming" within itself, it must re-examine both the simplified image of the boisterous Paddy and the elegant use of the English language; Friel puts it as follows:

> I think that is how the political problem of this island is going to be solved [...] It's going to be solved by the recognition of what language means for us on this island [...] Because we are in fact talking about accommodation or marrying of two cultures here, which are ostensibly speaking the same language but which in fact aren't[23]

Friel's final play *The Communication Cord* has to be read "in tandem" with *Translations*, in that it was written as a counterweight to the critics' solemn treatment of the previous work. It has the characteristics of a classical farce but is at the same time another exemplification of a linguistic theory. Whereas *Translations* postulates the need to renew the Irish linguistic contour, *Com. Cord* shows us what happens after the ancient tongue has completely gone and been replaced by one of conceit and pragmatism. The story's central character, Tim Gallagher, is writing a thesis on "Discourse Analysis with Particular Reference to Response Cries" in which he formulates two levels of communication: that of the exchange of information, and that of the realm of conversation. The latter, according to him, can only be reached if the two partners want to share each other's experience, that is, take off their masks and engage in sincere discourse. The whole play, then, functions as a complete annihilation of his premiss about speech: the protagonists are incapable of truthful verbal intercourse and use worn clichés, speak different tongues or confuse identities.

Looking back on what has been said so far, it seems plausible to conclude that Friel's unease with the English language points towards the dramatist's unease with his own creation and ultimately becomes a confession of his failure as an artist. Yet the author's uncertainty about

---

[22] *Selected Plays*, p. 439.
[23] Fintan O'Toole, "The Man from God Knows Where", p. 23.

his writing betrays more than an aesthetic-philosophical interest in the material of his work.

It is essentially a continuous search for a renewed creation of the self in its social and cultural dimensions. To put it differently, the crisis of the word in Friel's art cannot be separated from the problem of identity in Irish culture and by extension, from the sense of alienation in modern society. Like Synge, Joyce and O'Casey before him, he tries to find out what it means to be "Irish" and undermines old beliefs, berates social attitudes or views ancient traditions from a new perspective. It is a position of sceptical realism that results from his being a Catholic dramatist in Northern Ireland writing in the English language. Indeed, feeling all adrift in contemporary Ireland, he has been able to put age-old prejudices into question and to develop an objective concern for his culture. That is why the author strikes the reader as primarily interrogating the features determining Irish culture without offering clearcut answers. Showing what is wrong, he demythologizes some of the traditional illusions and forces us into a critical interpretation of the present. Through its subversive use of "myths" (e.g. the inversion of the Irish-English antithesis in *Translations*) Friel's theatre appears to be operating as a disquieting dramatization of his country's impotence to create a *true* image of itself, free from "the monotony of type" and "slavery of custom". If Ireland - and the North in particular - is to become politically mature, it must come to terms with its own (linguistic, social) history and take itself seriously. Furthermore, Friel's disengagement from dramatic convention - such as the split personality device in *Philadelphia*, the flash backs and outside commentators in *Freedom* - together with his reservations about present-day speech are essentially "stylistic" meditations on the way we define ourselves. Like Joyce, he believes that man can only find his own voice by allowing language its genuine freedom.

Ginette Verstraete

HISTORY IN THE POETRY OF DEREK MAHON

Although Derek Mahon has been rising toward major status during the last decade both as a poet and as a translator, his relatively small poetic output still deserves a wider international audience. Critical attention has not exactly been scant, but the problem is that some of the best criticism has appeared in small Irish periodicals or in Irish newspapers which are not readily accessible abroad[1], while some of the worst criticism is easily available on the stacks of our libraries. Robert Hogan's splenetic and schoolmasterly entry on Mahon in his *Macmillan Dictionary of Irish Literature* (1980) is a prime example of the latter, presenting Mahon as a poet of uncertain formal control in comparison with Auden. Mahon's "faulty examples of meter and rhyme" are cavilled about, and to cap it all Hogan does not hesitate to upbraid him for "still conducting his prosodic education in public" and for seeming "as untutored" as many of his generation (if more talented than most).

What is one to make of such a critical stance? The "obvious alternatives" are that Hogan himself does not adequately understand, or indeed does not "care for" what he is doing (to turn one of his other negative observations on Mahon against himself).

More perceptive critics such as Edna Longley noticed the "subtle brilliance" of Mahon's rhetoric as early as 1968[2], and in the last few years this has been corroborated by substantial essays exploring the cunning intricacies of Mahon's prosody. These remarkable contributions have included analyses of his disguising of rhyme patterns in apocopated and slant rhymes, as well as of the link between such prosodic technicalities as a recurrent anticlimactic rhyme scheme and a comparable movement in culture and history.[3] As an implicit rebuttal of Hogan's ill-informed criticism these recent essays are so perfect that further polemic is superfluous.

---

[1] E.g. Brendan Kennelly, "Lyric Wit", *Irish Times* Dec. 22, 1979 (dubbing Mahon "a Belfast Keats with a Popean sting"); Aidan C. Mathews, "Winter Quarters for a Poet-exile", *Irish Times* Feb. 19, 1983.

[2] In her review of *Night-Crossing (The Honest Ulsterman* No.8, Dec. 1968, p. 27-29).

[3] Dillon Johnston, *Irish Poetry after Joyce* (Notre Dame/USA: University of Notre Dame Press & Mountrath: Dolmen Press, 1985), p. 224-246; Edna Longley, "The Singing Line: Form in Derek Mahon's Poetry" in her *Poetry in the Wars* (Newcastle upon Tyne: Bloodaxe Books, 1986), p. 170-184.

However, there is also another type of criticism, as misdirected and preposterous as Hogan's but even more complacently silly, that has been doing a great disservice to a wider recognition of Mahon's achievement: namely, the crass Marxist approach as represented by Stan Smith. Although at least two critics have already in passing taken exception to his "unwise" and "inaccurate" criticism[4], this issue still seems less preempted than the formal one. Hence the focus of this contribution will be on Mahon's concept of history in some paradigmatic poems and its misrepresentation in both a review essay and a book by Stan Smith; special reference will be made to Walter Benjamin's philosophy of history throughout my argument.

The most superciliously negative criticism of Mahon from an ideological point of view was perpetrated by Smith in 1980 in a review essay significantly entitled "At One Remove"; this dealt with Mahon's *Poems 1962-1978* as well as Michael Longley's *The Echo Gate* and Maurice Harmon's anthology *Irish Poetry After Yeats*. Subsuming Mahon's multifarious output under the Procrustean category of "The Ulster Poem", Smith facetiously proceeds to define this sub-genre as "Tragical-comical-elegiacal-pastoral...":

"It makes a show of being terse, but is often wordy, even sententious. It performs its civic duties equitably, by reflecting, in an abstracted kind of way, on violence (...); but its hands are indubitably clean. For this it is always winning prizes, for it is competent poetry (...). It speaks, at times, with the tone of a shell-shocked Georgianism that could easily be mistaken for indifference, before the ugly realities of life, and death, in Ulster; at times, with the true voice of pastoral: it bleats. (...)
Sheepishly, it looks back to Louis MacNeice as its literary progenitor, like Derek Mahon in "Carrowdore Churchyard" (...); and it seeks to reproduce "Each fragile, solving ambiguity" of that older and more troubled poet."[5]

Further questionable labels inflicted on Mahon include "bone-bred parochiality" (without the positive meaning "parochial" had in Kavanagh's poetics), and moreover his "drained-off, privatized, self-indulgent" poetry is unfavorably compared with Montague's and Heaney's because "there is anger and ferocity in their response to the historic dilemma of the North, but no washing of hands in sanctimonious disdain".

---

4 Gerald Dawe: "Icon and Lares: Derek Mahon and Michael Longley", in: *Across a Roaring Hill. The Protestant Imagination in Modern Ireland*, eds. G. Dawe and E. Longley (Belfast: Blackstaff Press, 1985), p. 232; E. Longley (as in note 3), p. 173.
5 *Literary Review*, No.22, Aug.8, 1980, p. 11.

There is something utterly wrong with this kind of arid criticism, and the same holds true of Smith's discussion of Mahon in his book *Inviolable Voice. History and Twentieth-Century Poetry* (Dublin: Gill and Macmillan 1982, p. 188-193). Again Mahon's "uncomprehending stance" towards the Ulster dilemma is chidden, particularly his polarising of reality into the quotidian and the apocalyptic, resulting in the latter's reduction to mere fantasy -- and thereby ratifying a larger refusal of "the concept of history". It is very ironical that Smith tries to use ammunition from Walter Benjamin for a finishing shot at Mahon; such superficial appropriation of a thinker noted for his complexity and profundity is of course bound to backfire. Let us try to straighten out Smith's messy argument and see what we can gain from what is, one hopes, a less inadequate use of Benjamin's ideas.

Smith wants to play off Benjamin against Mahon by stressing the former's superior insight into what he perceives to be a similar historical process at work in Germany in the 1930s, as expressed in one of the "Theses on the Philosophy of History" (nr. VIII). Smith's quotation of this key text is, however, regretfully truncated and will in due time have to be restored to yield its full signifance:

"The tradition of the oppressed teaches us that the "state of emergency" in which we live is not the exception but the rule. We must attain to a conception of history that is in keeping with this insight. (...) The current amazement that the things we are experiencing are "still" possible in the twentieth century is not philosophical. This amazement is not the beginning of knowledge - unless it is the knowledge that the view of history which gives rise to it is untenable."[6]

Benjamin here implicitly refers to the Aristotelean concept of "thaumazein" as the potential beginning of all knowledge and differentiates it from the perplexity or panic of the late thirties which was not productive with a view to gaining insight into what was actually happening.

The latter attitude is also Mahon's today, Smith feels: remaining locked in a consumer's view of history, Mahon "steadfastly refuses Benjamin's perception".[7] This way of putting it implies a curious innuendo of obstinate ignorance or even bad faith, whereas there is no palpable evidence that Mahon actually read Benjamin either in the original or in the English translation of *Illuminationen* first published in

---

[6] *Inviolable Voice*, p. 192.
[7] *Inviolable Voice*, p. 193.

1968.[8] To be sure, there is little doubt that the latter volume circulated as a "Geheimtip" among leading members of the Irish avantgarde connected with the periodical *Atlantis* such as Seamus Deane, William J. McCormack, and Mahon himself. Also Mahon's translations of Brecht poems may have familiarized him with the concept of history shared to a certain extent by Benjamin and Brecht.

However, what some Marxist critics tend to overlook and even to suppress is that Benjamin's last works, including the "Theses", were written under the shadow of the infamous pact between Hitler and Stalin that betrayed him and so many other exiles. The "Theses" are a desperate attempt to reconcile materialism and Jewish mysiticism by discovering in the latter enough messianic drive to sustain the flawed spirit of the former in a period of danger and impending doom.[9] Overstressing one pole of Benjamin's thought, i.e. his radical materialism and his advocacy of class struggle, Smith obliterates certain fundamental affinities between Benjamin and Mahon in terms of utopian and messianic impulses and potentialities. Whether these affinities are cases of creative coincidence or whether Mahon is indebted to Benjamin directly or indirectly doesn't really matter; the point is that they may lead to mutual illumination.
To put the problem into perspective, the part of the VIIIth thesis elided by Smith needs first to be restored:

> "Then we shall clearly realize that it is our task to bring about a real state of emergency, and this will improve our position in the struggle against Fascism. One reason why Fascism has a chance is that in the name of progress its opponents treat it as a historical norm."[10]

In other words: Benjamin reacts against the ideology of linear progress which is not equipped to deal with throwbacks: he implies that it would be preferable to take catastrophe as a historical norm instead. This gloomy perspective is very close to Mahon's in many of his poems. On the other hand, however, Benjamin and Mahon share a basic desire to rescue and redeem whatever is worth saving in the world and in history, albeit often unrecognized by the "compact majority" as vitally

---

[8] Edited and with an introduction by Hannah Arendt; translated by Harry Zohn (New York: Harcourt Brace). Smith quotes from the 1973 Fontana/Collins edition, my references are to the 1970 Jon.Cape edition. With all due respect for Zohn's pioneering achievement, it remains nonetheless imperative to read Benjamin in German if one wants to appreciate the glimmering quality of his discourse.
[9] The best commentary is Irving Wohlfarth's "On the Messianic Structure of Walter Benjamin's Last Reflections", *Glyph* 3 (1978), p. 148-212.
[10] *Illuminations*, p. 263.

important for the survival of mankind or even entirely abandoned as a lost cause.

The most successful expression of this belief is to be found in an elegy from *The Snow Party* (1975) -- "arguably the finest poem to come out of Ireland in the past twenty years", as Declan Kiberd put it in 1982.[11] To realize the validity of this statement, it is indispensible to read the poem aloud in its entirety; only the most relevant parts can be quoted here.[12]

A DISUSED SHED IN CO. WEXFORD

Let them not forget us, the weak souls among the asphodels. - Seferis, Mythistorema

for J.G. Farrell

Even now there are places where a thought might grow -
Peruvian mines, worked out and abandoned
To a slow clock of condensation,
An echo trapped for ever, and a flutter
Of wildflowers in the lift-shaft,
Indian compounds where the wind dances
And a door bangs with diminished confidence,
Lime crevices behind rippling rainbarrels,
Dog corners for bone burials;
And in a disused shed in Co. Wexford,

Deep in the grounds of a burnt-out hotel,
Among the bathtubs and the washbasins
A thousand mushrooms crowd to a keyhole.

"Even now" may ring a bell for readers who remember the repeated topicalization of these words in the curious poem at the end of Steinbeck's *Cannery Row*, a novel celebrating the thriving Monterey of the Thirties of which only shadowy vestiges remain today -- thus implicitly reinforcing the pervasive atmosphere of global decay. But more importantly, at least for this reader, "Even now" can be linked to the Benjaminian concept of "Jetztzeit" (presence of the now), a cornerstone of his philosophy of history not unrelated to the mystical

---

[11] Review of *Poems 1962-1978*, *Irish University Review*, 12 (1982), No.1, p. 109.
[12] From the definitive version in *Poems 1962-1978* (Oxford: Oxford University Press, 1979; Second edition: 1986), p. 79-80. This poem has also been widely anthologized, e.g. in *The Penguin Book of Contemporary British Poetry*, eds. Blake Morrison and Andrew Motion, p. 79-80.

"nunc stans" but containing wider societal ramifications. Actually this concept was already implicitly present in the above quoted VIIIth thesis; the *real* state of emergency is in its revolutionary potential practically a synonym of the "Jetztzeit" as defined in the XIVth thesis:

> "History is the subject of a structure whose site is not homogeneous, empty time, but time filled by the presence of the Now (Jetztzeit). Thus, to Robespierre ancient Rome was a past charged with the time of the now which he blasted out of the continuum of history."[13]

Now Mahon, not being a Jacobin or a radical Marxist, does not blast open the continuum of history, but nevertheless in his own subdued way the does prize it open to look for something preserved, as it were, under a shell from the days of the Civil War -- something that might help to solve the problem of the Irish deadlock and the resurgent troubles of the late sixties.

Several critics have already emphasized the importance of the dedication to J.G. Farrell (1935-1979), whose novel *Troubles* (1970) is set in a fictitious village of County Wexford in the period 1919-21 when many Big Houses and hotels were burnt down. Although not generally recognized as a masterpiece, this novel is a remarkable example of the authentic historical novel as defined by Lukacs: "one which would rouse the present, which contemporaries would experience as their own pre-history".[14] It was only during the writing process that Farrell realized how relevant his topic had suddenly become again, and this relevance struck not only reviewers such as Elizabeth Bowen but had a catalytic impact on Mahon as well.

Beyond the emphatic homage to a favorite writer, however, the poem's location in Wexford may also be associated with a number of historical facts -- which makes it all the more imperative not to dislocate the setting to Co.Wicklow as Seamus Deane repeatedly does in his otherwise brilliant essay on Mahon.[15] First of all, many readers know that Wexford was the first Irish county to be colonized from England. Fewer readers will realize that the county is also rich in memories of the 1798 rising, but nevertheless this connotation is not

---

[13] *Illuminations*, p. 263.

[14] As pointed out by Ronald Binns in his excellent monograph *J.G. Farrell* (London: Methuen, 1986), p. 27. Binns quotes from Mahon's obituary for Farrell in *The New Statesman* (Aug. 31, 1979, p. 313) but is apparently not aware of the influence exerted on Mahon's poetry: only novels by William Boyd and Mary Jones are mentioned in this respect (p.9).

[15] "Derek Mahon: Freedom from History", in his *Celtic Revivals. Essays in Modern Irish Literature 1880-1980* (London: Faber, 1985), p. 162, 163.

irrelevant. In 1798 insurgent pikemen fought against overwhelming odds, and only in Ulster and Wexford was the rising widespread. We should also keep in mind that 1798 generally came to represent "a myth of the last chance", symbolizing the last real attempt by Irish Presbyterian and Catholic to make common cause.[16]

Such a cluster of topographical and historical associations constitutes what Mahon has defined as "a community of imagined readership" in an interview with Willie Kelly, where his sense of place is differentiated from Heaney's by its being less sure:

> Seamus is very sure of his place; I've never been sure of mine. My home landscape, and here I mean North Antrim where I spent most of my childhood holidays, and not Belfast where I was born, figures largely in my poems. Aside from these poems the place that the poetry occupies is not a geographical location; it's a community of imagined readership.
> Some of my poems don't take place anywhere in particular, others take place quite specifically, in Co.Wexford, or North Antrim.[17]

Even though perhaps not all of the above associations may belong to the "meaning" consciously intended by the author, still they can enrich the reading process and contribute to the poem's "significance" for us (to borrow a useful distinction from E.D.Hirsch's *Validity in Interpretation*).

Mahon's affirmation of a potentially redeeming growth of insight even in the most unlikely Irish places also implies a rebuttal of Smith's deprecatory characterization of him as merely a watered-down MacNeice. Not only does Mahon go beyond MacNeice in terms of formal achievement as well as exceeding him inhis capacity to transmit "a sense of dread"[18], there is also a greater sense of positive, realisable values in him (or at least in this particular poem). This can be made clear by a juxtaposition with MacNeice's famous "Valediction" (1934), where he denies the Irish all capability of genuine growth and consequently decides to resolve all emotional ties with his doomed fatherland:

> But no abiding content can grow out of these minds
> Fuddled with blood, always caught by blinds. (...)
> I will exorcise my blood
> And not to have my baby-clothes my shroud

---

16 See Terence Brown, *The Whole Protestant Community: The Making of a Historical Myth*, Field Day Pamphlet No.7, 1985.
17 "Each Poem for me is a New Beginning", *The Cork Review*, 2, 1981, No.3, p. 11.
18 S. Deane, *A Short History of Irish Literature* (London: Hutchinson, 1986), p. 242.

> I will acquire an attitude not yours
> And become as one of your holiday visitors,
> And however often I may come
> Farewell, my country, and in perpetuum...

The visitor motif also emerges in Mahon's penultimate stanza, but loaded with a much richer emotional resonance:

> A half century, without visitors, in the dark -
> Poor preparation for the cracking lock
> And creak of hinges. Magi, moonmen,
> Powdery prisoners of the old regime,
> Web-throated, stalked like triffids, racked by drought
> And insomnia, only the ghost of a scream
> At the flash-bulb firing squad we wake them with
> Shows there is life yet in their feverish forms.
> Grown beyond nature now, soft food for worms,
> They lift frail heads in gravity and good faith.

Mahon at least tries to rise up to his obligations when confronted with the collective yearning of the imprisoned mushrooms struggling for light, i.e. he gives them a voice to lament the solitude of history:

> They are begging us, you see, in their wordless way,
> To do something, to speak on their behalf
> Or at least not to close the door again.
> Lost people of Treblinka and Pompeii!
> "Save us, save us," they seem to say,
> "Let the god not abandon us
> Who have come so far in darkness and in pain.
> We too had our lives to live.
> You with your light meter and relaxed itinerary,
> Let not our naive labours have been in vain!"

In one of the most wonderful essays ever written by a poet about a fellow-poet, Seamus Heaney has managed to grasp this poem's complexity and plangency as follows:

> ... what gives the poem its sorrow and insight is the long perspective, an intimacy with the clay-floored foetor of the shed kept in mind and in focus from a point of detached compassion, in another world of freedom, light and efficiency. To reduce the mushrooms' lives and appetites to counters for the frustrations and desolations of lives in Northern Ireland is, of course, one of those political readings which is perfectly applicable, but we recognize that this allegorical approach ties the poem too neatly

into its place. The amplitude of its effects, its vault-filling resonance depend upon its displaced perspective. Those rooted helplessly in place plead with the capable uprooted visitor, be he poet or photographer, and it is in this pleading that we find the psychological as opposed to the political nub of the poem".[19]

On the basis of such an extraordinary felicitous poem we can show that Mahon is not only MacNeice's heir but also his disinheritor (albeit not deliberately, as he modestly remarked when asked about his perception of this filiation). Actually it seems to me that Mahon is closer to Auden here, a poet he did not as often mention among his formative influences as some others (Graves, Beckett, W.S.Merwin, even MacNeice...) but who is perhaps as inevitably present in Mahon's work and in twentieth century poetry generally as Milton was omnipresent in eighteenth century poetry. More specifically the above quoted passage reminds one of Auden's elegy on Freud (1940):

> but he would have us remember most of all
> to be enthusiastic over the night,
>   not only for the sense of wonder
> it alone has to offer, but also
>
> because it needs our love. With large sad eyes
> its delectable creatures look up and beg
>   us dumbly to ask them to follow:
> they are exiles who long for the future
>
> that lies in our power, they too would rejoice
> if allowed to serve enlightenment like him...

More than the slippery rhetoric of a politicized poem such as "Spain", the subdued diction of this elegy manages to convey the collective yearning of oppressed humanity, and Mahon equals Auden at his best in this respect -- except for the superfluous and melodramatic exclamation "Lost people of Treblinka and Pompeii!" which is more reminiscent of Audenesque diction of the mid-thirties.[20] Even without this emphatic

---

[19] *Place and Displacement. Recent Poetry of Northern Ireland* (s.l.: Trustees of Dove Cottage, 1985), p. 9.

[20] It would be precarious to go beyond this general suggestion of an intertextual relationship and to define its exact nature more precisely. Even such a sensible critic as Dillon Johnston, in his remarkable analysis of the later poem "The Hunt by Night", jumps to conclusions in this respect: "A revision in the first of these stanzas indicates how far Mahon has detoured to pay tribute to W.H. Auden" (o.c. as in n.3, p. 244). Mahon's denying of this assumption in a conversation with me does of course not preclude the possibility of an unconscious interaction, but at any rate this is not an example of intended homage. Another interesting case in point is Smith's detecting "a deliberate nod of acknowledgement" to Edward

explanation, most readers would have realized that the subject of the poem is the tragic plight of defenseless people struggling for the luminosity of redemption and that the mushrooms are merely a paradoxical symbol (after all fungi don't need light, as they lack chlorophyl). But this is just a minor flaw in an otherwise brilliant poem, whose merits are recognized even by Stan Smith.

However, in the final count Mahon's stance is sneeringly dismissed by Smith. In contrast to Heaney and Montague, who, according to Smith, may need to renounce the troubled ground of bomb-torn Belfast in order to complete their art, "...poets such as Longley and Mahon need to have their noses rubbed in it, if they are to survive as poets, and, possibly, *as men* (my italics, J.D.). The middle ground and the middle distance are not the place where thought may grow, or wisdom flourish."[21] Hindered by such dogmatic blinkers, Smith is unable to see the possibility of (re)reading the poem from a Benjaminian perspective, although Mahon's strategy of using an almost Benjaminian epigraph could already have served as an eye-opener. The quotation from Seferis -- "Let them not forget us the weak souls among the asphodels" implies that the danger of oppression persists even among the flowers covering the Elysian fields. This is consonant with Benjamin's view of history as expressed, for instance, in Thesis VI: "Only that historian will have the gift of fanning the spark of hope in the past who is firmly convinced that *even the dead* will not be safe from the enemy if he wins. And this enemy has not ceased to be victorious."[22]

Instead, Smith keeps harping on Mahon's "refusal of history", e.g. in "Autobiographies", a sequence of two poems in which childhood impressions are recaptured. Mahon's wonder at his own sheltered existence in a period when Jews were exterminated leads to the final verdict: "The distance of the fortunate beneficiary of victory is here faithfully inscribed"[23], a verdict which is at once harsh and smug. It is also self-defeating, as it exposes once more the critic's inability to relate to a writer's private dimension -- something Benjamin was eminently capable of, witness e.g. his shrewd observations on Marcel Proust (whom he also translated). This attentiveness, a core value of Benjamin's approach to literature as well as to history and to life generally, is perhaps what is most conspicuously and most sadly lacking in the criticism of his epigones fifteen years ago in Germany and now also in Britain.

Thomas's poem "Digging" in Seamus Heaney's poem with the same title (*Inviolable Voice*, p. 4). However, on Aug.23, 1986, Heaney told me that no such echo had been intended.

[21] *Literary Review*, p. 12.

[22] *Illuminations*, p. 257.

[23] *Inviolable Voice*, p. 193.

How then can the Proust-Benjamin connection be made productive for our purposes? Some felicitous formulations from Irving Wohlfarth's essay on Benjamin can clarify the issues involved. Taking his cue from Benjamin's observation that the idea of happiness is bound up with that of redemption, and that the same holds for the image of the past to which history gives its allegiance, Wohlfarth points out that such happiness would appear to be neither "hymnic" nor "elegiac", neither wholly unprecedented nor merely repetitive:

> Therein Benjaminian redemption differs from its Proustian model, which it quotes - and thereby completes - against its context. Unlike *mémoire involontaire,* which finds its fulfillment in the pure repetition of the past (...), the recuperation of the past that Benjamin intends is its restructuring completion, the fulfillment of its wishes. (...) In each case, individual and collective, the messianic light of redemption has the effect of retroactively articulating the past. Only with its fulfillment does the past fall into place; its completion coincides with its final reinterpretation. (...) And the rhythm of fulfillment is that of messianic actuality, the split second of the "fulfilled now"...[24]

Even though Mahonian redemption may differ from the Benjaminian model in some respects, basically they are consonant: in both cases the private and the public self merge to an extent which is not found in Proust.
In this context, the hitherto unnoticed autobiographical component of "A Disused Shed..." should be taken into account. The poem is indeed disguised autobiography in the most interesting sense, as we can gather from an interview with Paul Durcan:

> "In the back-garden there was a coal-shed in which Mahon kept his bicycle. (...) The little boy felt pity for the coal in the coal-shed and each time he closed the coal-shed door he felt regret, if not guilt. Why should all that glittering coal be shut away and live an imprisoned anti-social life of its own?"[25]

Although the link with "A Disused Shed..." is not explicitly made, the identity theme is of course fundamentally the same; it recurs in significant variations throughout Mahon's oeuvre, testifying to the pervasiveness of its autobiographical impulse.[26]

---

[24] Wohlfarth (as in n.9), p. 185.

[25] Paul Durcan, "The World of Derek Mahon", *Magill,* Christmas, 1984, p. 43.

[26] Thus lending support to Paul de Man's controversial thesis that autobiography is not a genre or a mode, but a figure of reading or of understanding that occurs,

In a less disguised way, the same childhood epiphany occurs in the title poem of the volume *Courtyards in Delft* (1981), contributing again to a highly interesting merger of the private and the public dimension. In fairness to Smith, it should be mentioned that this poem was not yet accessible to him at the time of his attacks; one hopes it will make him refrain from further ill-informed attempts at maligning Mahon as a petty bourgeois poet lacking in historical insight, for it is a perfect illustration of Benjamin's VIIth thesis:

> Whoever has emerged victorious participates to this day in the triumphal procession in which the present rulers step over those who are lying prostrate. According to traditional practice, the spoils are carried along in the procession. They are called cultural treasures, and a historical materialist views them with cautious detachment. For without exception the cultural treasures he surveys have an origin which he cannot contemplate without horror. They owe their existence not only to the efforts of the great minds and talents who have created them, but also to the anonymous toil of their contemporaries. There is no document of civilization which is not at the same time a document of barbarism."[27]

By "brushing history against the grain", as Benjamin defines the task of a historical materialist, Mahon tries in this poem to open the reader's eyes to the connections between a 17th century Dutch painting by Pieter de Hooch steeped in chaste precision, and the horrific expansion of the Dutch colonial empire.

The poem goes beyond a mere restatement of such uncomfortable knowledge as can already be found in didactic poems by Brecht in that Mahon adds a private dimension, exploring the analogy with his childhood environment and its comparable enmeshment of protestant cleanliness and delusions of imperialist vocation:

COURTYARDS IN DELFT
-Pieter de Hooch, 1659
(*for Gordon Woods*)

Oblique light on the trite, on brick and tile-
Immaculate masonry, and everywhere that
Water tap, that broom and wooden pail

---

to some degree, in all texts ("Autobiography As De-Facement", in his *The Rhetoric of Romanticism* (New York: Columbia University Press, 1984), p. 70).
[27] *Illuminations*, p. 258.

To keep it so. House-proud, the wives
Of artisans pursue their thrifty lives
Among scrubbed yards, modest but adequate.
Foliage is sparse, and clings. No breeze
Ruffles the trim composure of those trees.

No spinet-playing emblematic of
The harmonies and disharmonies of love;
No lewd fish, no fruit, no wide-eyed bird
About to fly its cage while a virgin
Listens to her seducer, mars the chaste
Precision of the thing and the thing made.
Nothing is random, nothing goes to waste:
We miss the dirty dog, the fiery gin.

That girl with her back to us who waits
For her man to come home for his tea
Will wait till the paint disintegrates
And ruined dykes admit the esurient sea;
Yet this is life too, and the cracked
Out-house door a verifiable fact
As vividly mnemonic as the sunlit
Railings that front the houses opposite.

I lived there as a boy and know the coal
Glittering in its shed, late-afternoon
Lambency informing the deal table,
The ceiling cradled in a radiant spoon.
I must be lying low in a room there,
A strange child with a taste for verse,
While my hard-nosed companions dream of war
On parched veldt and fields of rain swept gorse;

For the pale light of that provincial town
Will spread itself, like ink or oil,
Over the not yet accurate linen
Map of the world which occupies one wall
And punish nature in the name of God.
If only, now, the Maenads, as of right,
Came smashing crockery, with fire and sword,
We could sleep easier in our beds at night.[28]

---

[28] This definitive version is now the opening poem of *The Hunt by Night* (Oxford: Oxford University Press, 1982) (Second edition 1986-), p. 9-10.

For all his revolutionary fervour at the end of this poem, in which Mahon for a change blasts open the continuum of history in a genuinely Benjaminian spirit, the fact that the poet is deeply implicated is not denied with the superior detachment of the Brechtian stance. Rather like Benjamin, who also had an incurably ambivalent admiration for certain privileged works of art (such as Klee's "Angelus Novus") while concurrently trying to demystify their aura, Mahon realizes that he is addicted to art no matter how immoral its origins. It is doubtful whether his recent resolution to kick "the very bad habit" of writing poems about paintings will prove to be a lasting one.[29]

An almost insurmountable obstacle to negotiate for the average reader is of course that such a "connoisseur poem" is accessible only to the happy few who can visualize the Courtyard painting and the several paintings by Vermeer which are so lovingly described without being precisely identified.[30] There is indeed a contradiction between this elitist attitude and Mahon's reiterated affirmation that "the plain people of Ireland" will remain, in his view, the audience deciding what good poetry is all about.[31]

It is precisely this kind of unresolved tension and contradiction that makes following Mahon's career all the more fascinating.[*]

Joris Duytschaever

---

[29] Terence Brown, "An Interview with Derek Mahon", *Poetry Ireland Review*, No.14, Autumn 1985, p. 16-17.

[30] The extraordinary inspring power of these Vermeer paintings not only for poetry but also for critical theory is demonstrated in Claude Richard's article "Oedipa Regina", *Dires. Revue du centre freudien de Montpellier*, No.2, Janvier 1984, p. 67-84 (with reproductions).

[31] Interview as in n.29, p. 11.

[*] Grateful acknowledgment is made to Jennifer A. Otlet for her comments upon an earlier version of this article.

FINNEGANS WAKE IN IRISH LITERARY HISTORY*

> I write this under
> the injunction of *FW* 304. F3:
> 'Wipe your glosses with what you know.'

This is not so much my title as the heading under which I hope to raise some questions, attempt some comparisons, and initiate some debate. For in the beginning one should probably admit that *Finnegans Wake* does not exist within an Irish literary history. It has occupied, exclusively, an isolation thought to be splendid. Yet on the heels of that depressing observation follows the further admission that no Irish literary history of any complexity or extent has been written. All is, therefore, still to be determined - or liberated. Independent of any projected historical placing, Joyce's last great work has gradually been acknowledged as the conclusive, perhaps cancelling document of Irish modernism, a unique text drawing on but never drawing towards other texts. And beyond the exercise of comparing one work to another, there lies the larger issue of literary production, its various modes and the forces at work upon them.

I

We could of course begin by examining the extent to which *Ulysses* and *Finnegans Wake* cohere. A. Walton Litz early established the closeness in time of Joyce's final labours on the one and his commencement of work upon the other. Others have taken up his argument to good effect. The penultimate episode of *Ulysses* ends with phrases which anticipate something of the appearance of the *Wake's* language:

> Going to dark bed there was a square round Sinbad the Sailor roc's auk's egg in the night of the bed of all the auks of the rocs of Darkinbad the Brightdayler.[1]

This Brightdayler is not unknown to the 'lightbreakfastbringer' of the *Wake*'s Book III Chapter 2, but celebration of the connection is tempered by our knowledge that the *Wake* at this point is far from

---

* This paper was read at the Finnegans Wake Symposium at the University of Leeds on Tuesday, 14 July 1987.

[1] James Joyce, *Ulysses* [the corrected text] (London: Bodley Head, 1986), p. 607.

tempered by our knowledge that the *Wake* at this point is far from over: a more thorough awakening than that which hailed Shaun (in an early draft) as 'heart & soul of shamrogueshire' has yet to be earned.[2] There are, in other words, important lines of demarcation between the two novels. One of these underscores the distinction between time and history. *Ulysses* being distanced in history from its successor by the events of the Anglo-Irish war, the Treaty and the Irish civil war, in the period (roughly) from 1919 to 1923. To this historical and political situation of the *Wake* we shall, I hope, return.

Of course, literary history does not exclude a work's future, the literature it gives rise to in some sense. *Finnegans Wake* has its obvious legacy - the post-war novels of Samuel Beckett (especially the trilogy and *Comment c'est*) come to mind. But with apologies to Foxrock, one has to insist that this legacy (as much in Beckett's case as in that of Sollers) is French. An Irish literary historian, attempting to discuss the *Wake*'s Irish influence, is a bald man splitting hairs to prove his own identity. Post-war Irish fiction, Beckett apart, continued to pursue naturalistic and provincial objectives, and even in the case of Flann O'Brien (whose reputation has been much vaunted) the two complex novels both have their provenance in the late-1930s and the years very immediately following.[3] It is only in the slowly exposed work of Thomas Kinsella that any sustained relation to Joyce's last great endeavour can be discovered. Kinsella's early poetry is dominated by images of rigid and astronomically remote order. 'First Light', a poem collected in 1958, presents this in the lines:

> Stars ticked uncontrollably down
> The night-face, registering another
> Million routine stoops
> Into the kindling reeds, as quietly accomplished again.[4]

Indeed, 'register' is Kinsella's early preoccupation as much as the stars are, and it is not too much to argue that his inaugurating concerns are pre-registered in that catechistical entry of Joyce's 'Ithaca' which ends with 'the inanity of extolled virtue: the lethargy of nescient matter: the apathy of the stars'.[5]

---

[2] *A First Draft Version of Finnegans Wake*, ed. David Hayman, London, 1963, p. 227.

[13] The two novels are *At Swim-Two-Birds* (originally published in 1939) and *The Third Policeman* (posthumously published in 1967 and evidently composed shortly after the former). A number of lesser works intervene between these publication-dates.

[4] Thomas Kinsella, *Another September* (Dublin: Dolmen Press, 1962), p. 14.

[5] *Ulysses*, p. 604.

The significant swerve in Kinsella's development came with the publication of *Nightwalker and Other Poems* in 1968. The title poem enacts the writer's disenchantment with the political and economic changes of the decade: cameo descriptions of government ministers, German investors, and suburban connoisseurs were drawn explicitly in derivation from photographs. Notable among these was a wedding group snapped just before the opening of the Irish civil war, in which war the groom Kevin O'Higgins will judicially murder his best man only to be in turn assassinated by supporters of his principal guest: this fadograph had been republished in a popular history of Ireland since the Easter Rising and it was in this context Kinsella had encountered it. A second picture which worked its way into *Nightwalker* was of Charles J.Haughey in hunting pinks; Kinsella further embellishes the fox-hunter by mounting him on the Wakean 'big white harse' of the Willingdone. This detail is not merely opportunistic: the second section of the poem closes with the rubric 'Hesitant, cogitating, exit', and the whole poem with its re-living of the Civil War in the brutally new dispensation of Sean Lemass's Programme for Economic Expansion is framed between the blue trance of a television screen and an unnamed Joyce as 'Watcher in the tower' above the scrotum-tightening 'Sea of Disappointment'.[6] The entire composition might be summarised in a headline borrowed from Book One, Chapter Three: 'Television kills telephony in brothers' broil.' (*F W* 52.18)

The pattern is not abandoned. Kinsella's *Notes from the Land of the Dead* opens with a variation on his Wakean rubric: 'hesitate, cease to exist'.[7] The particular mutation, whereby 'exit' becomes 'exist' has its point but repeated variations of the verb to hesitate have a greater force in that behind them lies [sic] Richard Pigott's error in the spelling of hesitancy when he was in the witness box. This minor incident of Parnellite lore is of course familiar to devotees of *Finnegans Wake* through Joyce's incorporation of it in Book One, Chapter Two where HCE encounters the cad with the pipe while crossing the Phoenix Park. 'Hesitency was clearly to be evitated' (*F W* 35.20) on that occasion: not so with Kinsella whose work after *Nightwalker* has accumulated obscurity and a reputation for difficulty of which the author of the *Wake* could be proud. This obscurity, in both authors, is (I argue) a deliberate political tactic wholly consistent with the earlier tactics of silence, exile, and cunning; and, in the case of Thomas Kinsella, it should be read as a development of that seering

---

6 Thomas Kinsella, *Nightwalker and Other Poems* (Dublin: Dolmen Press, 1968), pp. 55-69.
7 Thomas Kinsella, *New Poems 1973* (Dublin: Dolmen Press, 1973), p. 9.

political analysis inaugurated in *Nightwalker*.[8] In a manner which the author of our latter-day 'polytropic man' must have approved, Kinsella is concerned to excavate the problematic of identity itself, and not just the personal or national trappings of same.

It is worth pausing to consider some of the circumstances which *Finnegans Wake* and the poetry of Kinsella's middle period share in some broad sense. I mean the immediate, Irish, political circumstances which today are probably more accessible than some of the periods of an earlier Irish history to which in due course I will turn. The *Wake* was written in exile by an Irish novelist personally invited by a minister in Ireland's first independent government to return home. It attends repeatedly to the fratricidal civil war, incorporates the nickname of the country's dominant politician (Dev) into the distinctive Wakean name of the capital city itself - Devlin. And it proceeds to embroider a dirtier, truer and funnier picture-book of Shamrogueshire than many which were banned by the mechanisms of censorship which were that government's real priority in cultural policy. In terms of domestic politics, *Finnegans Wake* had to be narratively obscure and etymologically inventive in order to evade the new nets thrown to trap the soaring spirit in the classic period of Irish national independence. That period is clearly over now, and it is part of Kinsella's significance as a poet that he sensed the inner collapse of the national being long before the revival of the 'brothers' broil' at the beginning of the 1970s. Of course that conflict has its own larger context also.

The Joyce of *Work in Progress* and the Kinsella of 'Worker in Mirror, at his Bench' are placed at opposite ends of the culture's spell as would-be-independent nation: neither is impressed by the efforts made or the values enshrined in the effort. In particular each attends to the ideology of union, unity, oneness, identity which underpins the assumption of national independence for a never-to-be-united Ireland. Each creates a complex and problematic critique of this urge towards homogeneity, whether the urge be directed towards the consolidation of the undifferentiated nation or towards the development of a consumer economy in which all classes are to be equipped with the same appetite for the same goods, with only purchase capacity distinguishing between them. Kinsella's procedures are less strictly inventive than Joyce's perhaps: in *One Fond Embrace* he summarises the new Dubliner's transformation of scrupulous meanness into conspicuous vulgarity in the generous line 'The Blue

---

8 See the present writer's rather constipated article "Politics or Community" in a special Kinsella issue of the magazine *Tracks*, No. 7, 1987, 61-77.

Nun is on me.'[9]   However, Joyce's own skilful deployment of the self-destructing cliché had reached its limit by the time he wrote 'Ithaca', and the language of *Finnegans Wake* sought different means to similar ends.

In the new work the word itself, which had come to be regarded as the epitome of self-bounded integrity, was to be shown in its interior diversity, with the layers of its real, pretended, and possible etymologies displayed almost in the manner of geological charts - but with the important difference from the charts that no particular layer was to be regarded, either materially or evaluatively as superior. But there is a further assumption that this procedure somehow puts Joyce in touch with an earlier, more dynamic etymological phase of linguistic development, an assumption which equates purity with proximity to roots: accordingly, the family-tree type of diagram is also employed to illustrate the 'descent' and 'proliferation' of words and languages from original, inaugurating elements. Both the geological and genealogical paradigms ignore - in varying proportions - the crucial role of print in the production of *Finnegans Wake*, the impossibility of this vast multi-layered text in any earlier mode of production, whether scriptal or oral. Thus the lexical item 'hered' in the question 'Have you hered?' (*FW* 44.18) represents (by not presenting) the absent English words 'heard' and 'here' and creates a past tense for the adverb 'here' (which is a hononym of 'hear') while also commencing the word 'hereditary' and visibly avoiding the lumpen 'herd'. This single lexical item, in other words, is irreducibly plural. And while one facet of the item may have a priority with most readers, no hierarchy of layers - to mix metaphors - is established. Few readers will, for example, have noticed that the item 'here' in Hungarian variously means testicle or shamrock!

'Have you hered?' is a comparatively minor instance of the *Wake*'s method. Just above it there are two sentences which, while they manifest little enough by way of syntactical or lexical invention, get to the heart of the matter:

> Some vote him Vike, some mote him Mike, some dub him Llyn and Phin while others hail him Lug Bug Dan Lop, Lex, Lax, Gunne or Guinn. Some apt him Arth, some bapt him Barth, Coll, Noll, Soll, Will, Weel, Wall but I parse him Persse O'Reilly else he's called no name at all. (*FW* 44.10-14)

At one level, what is established here is the ever-changing cognomen of the central figure, sometimes Here Comes Everybody, sometimes

---

9 Thomas Kinsella, *One Fond Embrace* (Dublin: Gallery Press, 1981), p. 13.

Haveth Childers Everywhere. Perhaps 'established' is not the term to use, however, for the infinite extension of the figure's names (everybody-where) rules out any simple identification of a single central figure. The Viking element in 'Vike' is easily placed, and Lex and Lax neatly partner each other, but the seemingly individualised name 'Persse O'Reilly' is offered only because 'else he's called no name at all'. Where have Gunne and Guinn gone? And who is the 'I' who offered the name of Persse O'Reilly in the first place, a name which fails to make an entry in the ballad named after him? Has the ballad lost an I, its authoring I?

The question of the identity of a dreamer in the *Wake* has consumed a good deal of time. Today it is fashionable to gloss the crisis of the Irish state in terms of rival identities - British/Irish, Protestant/Catholic etc. This use of the term 'identity' is undoubtedly sloppy, but maybe that has its own propriety. Maud Ellmann has pointed out that, in the second chapter of the *Wake*, the name of the father cannot be 'traced back to an originary fulness of identity.' And on the topic of identity generally, she notes the disagreement of etymologists as to whether the word 'derives from the Latin *idem*, meaning "the same"; or *identimem*, which means "over and over again, repeatedly" ...'[10] Identity, that is, has non-identical or at least rival origins, which is to say that it has no origin other than in the mode of production from which identity-theory proceeds. A very recent writer on the *Wake*, John Bishop, has elaborated the political and economic implications of the modern sense of personal identity - its generation of terms 'heavily invested with a sense of the "proper" and "propriety", of "ownership" and one's "own" ... that ensure adaptive survival within a system structured on the values of "possession" and "property"'.[11] Of course, the connection between these values and the rise of the novel was made long ago, but in Joyce's case we should note his determined and sustained effort to write, as it were, an *exploded reading* of the language (English) through which independent Ireland was both tied to these ideological values and frustrated in its attempt to assimilate them wholly to itself. Ireland, that is, was compelled by the hegemony of the English language to follow the path of a limited capitalist development, but never to reach a point on that path so advanced as to challenge the hegemony of British capitalism. In Book III Chapter 3, Joyce gives us a kaleidoscope of such a politico-linguistic travesty:

---

[10] Maud Ellmann, "Polytropic Man: Paternity, Identity and Naming in *The Odyssey* and *A Portrait of the Artist as a Young Man*" in *James Joyce; New Perspectives*, ed. Colin MacCabe (Brighton: Harvester Press, 1982), pp. 73-104, see p. 81.
[11] John Bishop, *Joyce's Book of the Dark: Finnegans Wake* (Madison: University of Wisconsin Press, 1985), p. 142.

And the three shouters of glory. Yelling halfviewed their harps.
Surly Tuhal smiled upon drear Darthoola: and Roscranna's
bolgaboyo begirlified the daughter of Cormac. The soul of
everyelsesbody rolled into its olesoleself(...) It was joobileejeu
that All Sorts' Jour. Freestouters and publicranks, hafts on
glaives. You could hear them swearing threaties on the
Cymylaya Mountains, man. (*FW* 329.15-19 and 30-33)

Here, MacPherson's forged Ossianic gallantry merges with thc civil
war of Free Staters and Republicans, in a passage not untinged (I
believe) by a self-mocking echo of Davin's encounter with the bare-
breasted woman in the Ballyhoura Mountains. The polytropic hero and
the polytropic text are potentially reduced to a species of
undifferentiated accommodation - 'everyelsesbody rolled into its
olesoleself' - which threatens to annihilate difference and mediation.
It is against this false elimination of difference that *Finnegans Wake*
repeatedly strives, and the slogans of national unity, independence,
and the harmony of social classes are potent forms of this reductive
homogeneity.

II

Our objective, however, is to locate the *Wake* in a literary rather
than an exclusively political Irish history. In order to do that it is
necessary to say something a little more specific about the book itself,
the kind of book it is, and the kind of material it is concerned with.
There is no point in pursuing the line of recognisable Irish texts which
appear and disappear in the course of the *Wake*; that approach has
been satisfactorily adopted by James Atherton and others who have
followed him. Instead of elaborating further affinities or analogies
between *Gulliver's Travels* or *Tristram Shandy* or *The House by the
Churchyard* and Joyce's last great novel, I hope to show the
advantages to be gained by considering one or two texts which we
may be fairly certain Joyce knew nothing of. After all, though
Finnegans Wake itself is a text of sleeping, of the unconscious mind, its
composition proceeded exclusively during the author's waking hours,
and the use of Le Fanu or Sterne is usually demonstrably logical and
deliberate. The book is a consciousness of unconsciousness, and thus
possesses an analogical relation to the operations of critique upon
ideology. In *Joyce's Book of the Dark* John Bishop has examined with
quiet authority this important feature of the novel. In this connection
one can quote as paradigmatic of the *Wake* as a whole the function of
Shem the Penman.

giving unsolicited testimony on behalf of the absent, as glib as eaveswater to those present (who meanwhile, with increasing lack of interest in his semantics, allowed various subconscious smickers to drivel slowly across their fichers), unconsciously explaining, for inkstands, with a meticulosity bordering on the insane, the various meanings of all the different foreign parts of speech he misused ... (*FW* 173.29-36)

It is worth noting here that the account of Shem's misuse of foreign words is itself almost devoid of those 'misused' or illegally imported lexical constructions thought typical of *Finnegans Wake*, the notable exception being the neologism 'fichers'. McHugh's *Annotations* has little or nothing to offer on the lines quoted, though it draws our attention not only to the standard English word 'features' (i.e. the human face) but also to the reflexive French verb 'se ficher' - to laugh at, to regard with indifference. The visual domain, reflectively the face of the sleeper, is thus discounted and the transaction highlighted by being thrown into isolated neologism. In brief, the *Wake* sets up no difficulty in describing its processes in relation to the language of dreams, and does not require that language for the purpose. I make this point because it is germaine to my principal endeavour which is to show how *Finnegans Wake* can be located in a literary history which extends well beyond the intertextual pale of the novel itself. Joyce can, in other words, easily accomodate that of which he had no knowledge. Though his concern is more strictly textual, Bishop is not in disagreement with my strategy; indeed he introduces a useful Hegelian emphasis on negation as motive power. Accordingly:

> to reconstruct that part of life lived in immobility and dream void sensory paralysis ... Joyce necessarily devises in *Finnegans Wake* a whole strange language of negation, a system of reference to no experience, whose infinitely inflected terms, equally signifying the absence of perception and the perception of nothing, ultimately replicate from his own "eyewitdless foggus" the "one percepted nought" endured by a man unconsciously drifting towards sunrise through "Real Absence".[12]

That Real Absence of course comes in many varieties. Early in Book One we read that 'To part from Devlin is hard as Nugent knew' (*FW* 24.25-26). The industrious McHugh informs us that Joyce here alludes to Gerald Nugent's 'Ode Written on Leaving Ireland' and quotes its line 'From thee, sweet Delvin, must I part.' The allusion, however, is both present and absent in *Finnegans Wake*, for the poem

---

[12] Ibid. p. 48.

was originally written in Gaelic, and rendered into Victorian sing-song English by William Hamilton Drummond. Joyce undoubtedly encountered the translation in the first edition of Read's *Cabinet of Irish Literature* - it is not in the second - published in 1879.[13] I say 'Victorian English' because the poem was originally written about 1607, and thus is remote historically as well as linguistically from the idiom alluded to here.[14] Moreover, Nugent wrote of leaving *Delvin*, a barony in County Meath to which the Nugent family was attached by noble title. In a sense a Nugent was a Delvin, indeed the poet's brother was Richard, 14th Baron Delvin. Moreover, Delvin (Dealbhna, in the original) is not only a metonymic rendering of Ireland, it derives from an eponymous personal name from which the population-group and hence district take their names. The Gaelic text is prolific in further such metonymic names - Banba, [Innis] Fail, Ir, etc. ... Joyce, on the other hand, has transformed the place-name into one of his versions of Dublin, Dubh Linn, Devlin. And on one occasion when Delvin does make a modified appearance in the *Wake*, the associations are explicitly those of a primal, undifferentiated world:

> It was of a night, late, lang time agone, in an auldstane eld, when Adam was delvin ... (*FW* 21.5-6)

The poem, in Gaelic and in English translation had once appeared in print prior to 1879: James Hardiman included it in the second volume of his *Irish Minstrelsy* of 1831, where it immediately followed after the classic Fenian poem, 'Is aoibhinn a bheith a m-Beinn-Eadar', with its express topographic tribute to Howth (Beann Eadar) as the location of Fionn's (Finn in the translation) recreational exploits. If Joyce didn't use Hardiman's *Irish Minstrelsy*, he managed to avoid an anthology which brought together the supreme Gaelic evocation of Howth and the isolated Nugent lament quoted in Book I, Chapter 1 of the *Wake*.[15] Incidentally, Gerald (or Garrett) Nugent's brother, William Nugent, wrote poems in Gaelic, sonnets in English, and virtually invented a new genre in Gaelic literature, the poem on departing into exile.[16] Their father had a varied career: in 1567, he was given a royal commission to extirpate the O'Mores, by 1574 he was in bad odour with the government, in 1580 he was imprisoned in

---

[13] *The Cabinet of Irish Literature*, eds G.A. Read and T.P. O'Connor (London: Blackie, 1879), vol.1, p. 8.

[14] See Paul Walsh, *Gleanings from Irish Manuscripts* (Dublin: Three Candles Press, 1933), 2nd ed., pp. 3-11, for a discussion of the poem, accompanied by a prose translation into English.

[15] *Irish Minstrelsy, or Bardic Remains of Ireland with English Poetical Translations*, ed. James Hardiman (London: Robins, 1831), vol.2, pp. 222-229.

[16] Eamonn O Tuathail, "Nugentiana", *Eigse*, vol.2. (1940), pp. 5-14, esp. pp. 11-13 for texts.

the Tower of London and he died in 1602, a prisoner in Dublin Castle. Nevertheless, in a letter to Burghley in 1591 he gave his favourite occupations, *Who's Who* style, as "books and building". *His* mother was one of the St. Lawrence family, lords of Howth, and in his will he appointed (among other executors) 'my cozen the lord of Howth that now is ...'[17]

The interrelation of all these families in the Elizabethan Pale is doubtless more obvious to modern historians than it might have been to Joyce with his Irish Victorian sense of what the past had been. Decisively, however, the unity of person and place in 'Adam was delvin', 'the Nugents of Delvin', and in the construction of Dealbhna, is strikingly absent from this comment on absence and emigration in the *Wake*, the locus of presence/absence being a seemingly unique Gaelic poem written by one who wrote only one poem. The apparently seamless integrity of that which is lamented in the poem is nowhere countenanced in *Finnegans Wake*, though by means of *FW* 21.6 Joyce has indicated the expulsion of 1607 has an Adamic analogue. The more innovative Nugent of the exile poems is appropriately missing. Yet the Real Absence of such figures as Garratt and William Nugent ... the Flight of the Earls, the Wild Geese, the boys in Botany Bay, the Tammany Hall gang, the Irish Centre in York Street ... is a dimension of the cultural milieu from which Joyce came. Indeed it is one which he consciously imitated and repeated, 'Remembering thee, O Sion.'[18] Absence exercises a pressure on that which is, and often the pressure is one of attraction. Attraction, or desire, would be cancelled by Presence. It is a theme repeatedly investigated in nineteenth-century Irish fiction, especially in the long line of novels deriving from Maria Edgeworth's *Absentee* (1812).

Joyce's arrogant remark to Samuel Beckett - "I can do anything with language I want" - carries with it a Herculean counterbalance, an obligation to do what has not been done before.[19] His impatience with what he had achieved in *Ulysses* need not be taken too seriously at the personal level and still be recognised as the signal of an important watershed in his treatment of language. There *is* a difference between the two novels, a difference as essential and obvious as that between day and night. Such a hiatus, or metamorphic arrest, occurs between periods or phases of culture, and Joyce elucidated the change he was engaged upon by comparing the classic and modern approaches to literature. There survive in the Bodley Library some fragmentary

---

17 "Nugent Papers" [a calendar], *Analecta Hibernica*, No. 20 (1958), p. 133.
18 *Ulysses*, p. 37.
19 See Richard Ellmann, *James Joyce* (New York: Oxford University Press, 1982), p. 702. (Quoted by Patrick Parrinder in *JJames Joyce* (Cambridge: Cambridge University Press, 1984), p. 200.)

notes of Edgeworth's, which I associate with her preparation of *The Absentee*, in which a comparable problem is discussed. Her principal concern is the nature and operation of literary allusion. With apologies for the disconnectedness of notes not prepared for publication, here are some of the relevant phrases:

> Popular writer must be regulated in choice of allusions by the actual state of knowledge in his country - Early poets confined to the striking and obvious phenomena of nature - As arts & sciences diffuse themselves orators and poets take from these their most elegant allusions - especially as they do not like to say the same things as have been said by their predecessors, about sunset & sunrise etc - The great appearances of nature have been described till there can be no longer any novelty in allusions to them - but the varieties & novelties of science & art are inexhaustible - ... Allusions by a single word sometimes show that a man has been in Arcadia - ... [20]

A realisation that the literary trope is susceptible to exhaustion is not of course original in Edgeworth, and indeed much of what I have transcribed here could be paralleled in the more connected critical essays of her contemporaries in the romantic generation. But Edgeworth displays no incipient longing for the organicist philosophies of literature then in preparation. What she evidently seeks is a radical alteration of the proportions, the structural relations, of allusion *per se*, in order to avoid the mechanically repetitive phrase which was almost simultaneously being named "stereotype" after the printing process singled out as the wicked perpetrator of this linguistic exhaustion.[21] Confronted with a crisis in the possibility of saying anything about the sunrise, she does not look back to some earlier dispensation when access to the sunrise was (allegedly) more direct. Similarly Joyce, near the close of *Ulysses*, moves beyond the comically deployed clichés of "Eumaeus" to develop the more intricately and materially structured language of *Work in Progress*, in the course of which "allusions by a single word" are raised to the n-th power.

---

[20] Bodley Library, Oxford, (Ms. Eng. misc. e. 1463). The notes entire appear as an appendix to the Worlds Classics edition (ed. W.J. Mc Cormack and Kin Walker) of Edgeworth's *The Absentee*.

[21] For a time-table linking use of "stereotype" in the commentary of Coleridge to the development of a theory of Anglo-Irish literature, see W.J. Mc Cormack, "'The Protestant Strain': Or, a Short History of Anglo-Irish Literature from S.T. Coleridge to Thomas Mann" in *Across a Roaring Hill: the Protestant Imagination in Modern Ireland*, eds Gerald Dawe and Edna Longley (Belfast: Blackstaff, 1985), pp. 48-78.

This is not the sole point on which Edgeworth and Joyce might provide the substance of a revealing comparison. Edgeworth refers to the necessity of the popular writer's regulating his language in accordance with "the actual state of knowledge in his [sic] country". But her fiction is eloquent testimony to the difficulty, perhaps even the impossibility of knowing what one's country was. In *Ennui* (1809), the bored English traveller in Ireland discovers that he is, in actuality, not the landlord he thinks he is but that landlord's foster-brother. The plot resolution in all of these novels - and the base is laid down as early as Sydney Morgan's *Wild Irish Girl* (1806) while the inverted apex of the pattern is reached in W.B. Yeats's *John Sherman* (1891) - the plot resolution, I say, is the imposition of fixity by marriage upon an alternating analysis of the elements conjoined in the *Union*, the United Kingdom of Great Britain and Ireland which lasted from 1801 to some time c. 1920 or 1921 (depending on your politics). Edgeworth's *The Absentee* is the epitome of this restless inquiry into the experience of absence, its hero sent several times out of England to Ireland, and back from Ireland to England. But, to return to at least one particular detail of *Finnegans Wake*, the historically sustained and sexually charged absence of Edgeworth's novel is vested in the heroine, whose name is Nugent. *The Absentee* strives to reverse the banishment signalled in Gerald Nugent's "Ode Written on leaving Ireland" by enacting the return of Grace Nugent as bride-to-be of the hero Lord Colambre. In a manner too prolix for summary here, the name Nugent signals absence, the character Nugent endures exile, and this throughout a cultural history of several centuries' duration.[22] "To part from Devlin is hard as Nugent knew" (24.25-26) may indeed allude to the Gerald Nugent who wrote the "Ode"; it equally well alludes to his father who died in "Devlin Castle" or to that Christopher Nugent who commanded a jacobite regiment at Ramillies, to his namesake who was Edmund Burke's father-in-law, to the field-marshall Laval Count Nugent who was the Wilingdone's Austrian ally against Napoleon. Nugents were perhaps the most notable family of "Wild Geese" émigrés in Europe. Their graves litter the continent.

There are other points of resemblance between *The Absentee* and *Finnegans Wake*. Each, for example, depends upon the currency of a popular song to provide a recognisable statement of a theme also expressed at less immediately accessible levels. By equally economical allusions, Edgeworth uses the biblical *Book of Esther* and an episode from Herodotus to underpin the incidents of her contemporary fiction. If Joyce developed the technique of "stream-of-consciousness" as a mode of narration, Edgeworth can take credit for the early use in

---

[22] See W.J. Mc Cormack, *Ascendancy and Tradition in Anglo-Irish Literary History from 1789 to 1939* (Oxford: Clarendon Press, 1985), pp. 136-153, 404-405. Also the introduction to *The Absentee* (see note 20 above).

English of "free indirect style", a technique which in *The Absentee* is employed to suspend, as it were, the audible presence of characters by providing the merely formal apparatus of their quoted speech but inserting in it the further formality of the writer's *oratio obliqua*. More substantially then, each novel is about absence. Joyce announced his objective succinctly enough:

> A nocturnal state, lunar. That is what I want to convey: what goes on in a dream, during a dream. Not what is left over afterwards, in the memory. Afterward nothing is left.[23]

The announcement is not without its epistemological problems, of course. But the notion of an *obliterated negative* is serviceable, the *Wake* a comprehensive representation of the wholly absent rendered intelligible by the systematic yet incomplete obliteration of its negation by language. Here I beg to difer from one emphasis made by John Bishop who at one point distinguishes radically between Wakese and English, the latter (in his view) conveying "meaning in its ideal form by indicating the presence of corresponding ideas and things".[24] Bishop himself has gone a long way to demonstrate how Joyce's novel employs a language of oppositional negation which, I believe, can yet be shown to preserve the dialectical potential of language in an age of mystical positivism. To draw on a distinction familiar in the jargon of semantics, *Finnegans Wake* relates to unconsciousness not by way of metaphor but by that of metonymy.

The absence of Edgeworth's novel cannot be glossed simply as emigration, the Irish abroad. Indeed that seemingly obvious sociological topic has to wait until the middle decades of the twentieth century before it finds any sustained literary expression in Ireland. No, *The Absentee* is concerned with two kinds of displacement and their potential reconciliation with each other. The hero Lord Colambre lives in London with his feckless parents, Lord and Lady Clonbrony: their absence from Ireland (from the place Colambre and the place Clonbrony which name them) is wholly voluntary, a full gesture of allegiance to fashion and centralised power. The heroine Grace Nugent, on the other hand, lives by toleration and necessity in her Clonbrony relatives' house. Her status is not fully determined: she is a dependent, her family (especially her mother) has transgressed in some way which is repeatedly summarised in the cryptic phrase that none of them were "sans peur et sans reproche". This accusing heraldic motto comes to the hero's mind whenever he tries to think of

---

[23] Quoted by Jacques Mercanton in *Portraits of the Artist in Exile: Recollections of James Joyce by Europeans*, ed. Willard Potts (Seattle: University of Washington Press, 1979), p. 207.

[24] Bishop, p. 51.

his desirable cousin. Even in the fashionable circles of London, ways are devised to avoid Grace Nugent, expressly to avoid her name, her presence in the text. Two gossips at a party discuss her abilities but find that her name constantly intrudes:

> "Two names already - did not I warn ye?"
> "But how can I make myself intelligible?"
> "Intials - can't you use - or genealogy?"[25]

Those to whom the allusion enacted in the name Grace Nugent is familiar will know that the early eighteenth-century harper composer Turlough Carolan composed numerous songs for members of the Nugent family, that these repeatedly allude to the family's enforced residence abroad as Jacobite supporters, to their likely return. The song "Grace Nugent" is simply the best known of these. Thus the absence signalled in the novel's heroine is wholly involuntary, historical rather than fashionable in its motive causes. Moreover, when hero and heroine finally return to Ireland, with the sound of wedding-bells not inaudible, they are greeted with a strikingly divided representation of what Grace's absence has entailed. First, to Grace Nugent is presented a young girl named Grace - there is much emphasis on namesakes. Second, a blind harper plays the song "Grace Nugent" though not a word of it is admitted to contest the returned heroine's presence. Now the historical conflict embodied in such songs is absented, in favour of a reconciliation between the dis-graced past and the recently disgraceful absentees.

III

Compared to Jonathan Swift or even Sheridan Le Fanu, Maria Edgeworth is a non-entity in the register of *Finnegans Wake* sources. Yet to take this measure of things is to remain within the domain of the controlling author's conscious decisions, his *choice* of sources. The consideration of *The Absentee* can help to remind us that there are, inevitably, unchosen sources. One such can be noted in passing. The six-volume *Collection of Poems by Several Hands* published by Robert Dodsley in 1758 contains in its second volume a sprightly poem by Robert, the earl Nugent, entitled "Epistle to Pollio, from the Hills of Howth in Ireland" in which compensation for withdrawal from the delights of the metropolis is guaranteed:

> Shou'd perchance some high-born fair,
> Absent, claim thy tender care;

---

[25] *The Absentee*, p. 38.

> Here enraptur'd shalt thou trace,
> S -- 's shape and R - 's face;
> While the waking dream shall pay,
> Many a wishing, hopeless day.[26]

In 1787, one Abraham Bosquet published "Howth, a descriptive Poem". *FW* 523.25 not withstanding, I think Joyce was unaware of this piece, almost everyone (happily) is.[27] These are trivial omissions on Joyce's part, and there are larger instances to be considered. The latter might be termed structural rather than textual sources, and their extent is unpredictably great. One is tempted to define them as analogies free of any suspicion of influence consciously registered in Joyce or his text. Lucien Goldmann's category of the homological also springs to mind - but for the fact that the "world view" encountered through these texts (including *Finnegans Wake*) is in each case irreducibly plural, and exists in a complex of iconic gesture and economic profusion. For the remainder of this paper I will concentrate on one such structural source and its significance in the development of an Irish literary history which does not enshrine *Finnegans Wake* by excluding it. But before taking up that task, I'd like to place on record a long-delayed project to which the present inquiry is clearly relevant. That is the relationship between changes in class structure and the forms of Irish prose fiction. In the English context, Ian Watt's elaboration of the interconnectedness of bourgeois development and the "rise of the novel" is well known, and with some later modifications and extensions, remains substantially in place. Watt is aware of Joyce and declares *Ulysses* to be "in so many ways the climax of the novel's development"; however, his more precise comments must surely raise problems and eyebrows:

> in its last two books the graphic presentation of Molly Bloom's daydream and the cataloguing of the contents of her husband's drawers are defiantly unadulterated examples of the adjustment of narrative manner to the subjective and objective poles of dualism.[28]

What drawers are these? And is not "unadulterated" an adjective only the narrator of "Eumeus" would have applied here? I draw attention to this lapse of Ian Watt's because I think it exemplifies the difficulty

---

[26] Robert Dodsley (ed.) *A Collection of Poems ... by Several Hands* (London: J. Dodsley, 1775), vol 2, pp. 207-210.

[27] Abraham Bosquet, *Howth, a Descriptive Poem* (Dublin: P. Byrne, 1797), see line 211:
> "Up her free port, her bloated navies glide ..." (p. 16)

[28] Ian Watt, *The Rise of the Novel: Studies in Defoe, Richardson and Fielding* (Harmondsworth: Penguin, 1972), p. 336.

Joyce presents to anyone attempting a comprehensive statement about the English language novel and bourgeois dualism, the relation between the individual and his environment. Joyce places a strain on certain categories and conclusions, and the strain sometimes is unconsciously given a comic turn of phrase. We know that Joyce was himself sufficiently interested in these problems to give a lecture in Trieste on Daniel Defoe. Between these two minor details - Watt's laughable aside and Joyce's isolated foray into English criticism - we should note a more serious omission, the absence from *The Rise of the Novel* of any reference to *Gulliver's Travels*. Now I am not anxious to make a case for *Gulliver's Travels* as a belatedly acknowledged member of the novel tribe. On the contrary, what is crucial is the manner, degree, and direction of its distant but actual bearing upon the development of the novel. I have argued elsewhere that though it cannot be classified as a novel, it is in some ways more than a novel, it goes beyond the limitations within which the fiction of Defoe and Fielding was to flourish and that in so doing it is valuably reflexive, almost indeed a meta-novel. In particular, its obsession with the procedures and implications of *classification* give it a crucial placing in the argument concerning the relationship of genre and class.[29]

Gulliver's Travels, composed in that most politically tense margin of the Augustan empire known as Ireland, shines its beacon of light penetratingly into the ideological presuppositions of Walpole's dispensation *and* those of Walpole's implicit critics. So too, I would suggest, *Finnegans Wake* stands in relation to English-language modernism, as a critique and a challenge to that movement's assumed position in literary history. In particular, its highly structured arrangement of four books, with their subordinate chapters, should be noted as an affront to the undifferentiating homogeneity which critics as different as T.S. Eliot and György Lukács ascribe to Joyce's accepted world. Eliot famously spoke of "the immense panorama of futility and anarchy which is contemporary history", Lukács of "aimless and directionless .... fields of force".[30] Eliot secretly fears Joyce's impact upon class, Lukács too prematurely assumes its abolition. Though the pressure of time here today requires us speedily to "go on backwards a little" (Beckett's phrase) in considering the larger issue of *Finnegans Wake* in Irish literary history, the mediation which the *Wake* effects in relation to modernism and alterations in class society do require a

---

29 See W.J. Mc Cormack, "On *Gulliver's Travels*" in Jeremy Hawthorn (ed.) *Narrative from Malory to Motion Pictures* (London: Edward Arnold, 1985), pp. 70-84.

30 T.S. Eliot, "*Ulysses*, Order, and Myth" in *Selected Prose of T.S. Eliot*, ed. Frank Kermode (London: Faber, 1975), p. 177; Georg Lukács, *The Meaning of Contemporary Realism* (trans. John and Necke Mander (London: Merlin Press, 1963), p. 18.

final emphasis. If we began by drawing attention to the book's proximity to the Irish civil war, this should be urgently counterbalanced by an acknowledgement of its role in the Europe of the 1930s and after. Writing in exile during the Second World War, Theodor Adorno was able already to predict the succession of fascism by a conspicuously well-equipped collectivist order in which "even Kafka is becoming a fixture in the sub-let studio" and to perceive - more trenchantly:

> That the hygienic shop-floor and everything that goes with it, the people's car or the sportsdrome, leads to an insensitive liquidation of metaphysics, would be relevant; but that in the social whole they themselves become a metaphysics, an ideological curtain behind which the real evil is concentrated, is not irrelevant.[31]

This kind of Germanic declaration has not been popular in the criticism of Anglo-Irish literature, perhaps because it has been absent from English criticism. In prompt support of Adorno's proposition, let us note carefully a particular transformation within the text of the *Wake*, that occurring between *FW* 164.31-32 and *FW* 237.28-29: the first passage refers to Signorina Cuticura and Herr Harlene - Cuticura and Harlene being proprietary cosmetics - and the second (by reverse spelling) creates seeming-divinities out of the Egyptian Book of the Dead, Aruc Ituc and Enel Rah. *Finnegans Wake* takes its place in a culture of resistance to such homogenising developments which Adorno elswhere acknowledged, and Beckett's *Endgame* was a work Adorno specifically analysed to exemplify this ability of literature - even after the war - to show how "the rising collectivist order is a mockery of a classless [society]."[32]

We have, however, lingered too long in the near-present and must get on our way. Let me at once accelerate and concentrate your attention by drawing it to a work published in 1871 under the title *The Book of Howth* and commencing thus:

> The genealogy of Fin Herin came out of Denmark, and landed at Falis-ni-Grye Barrerove whose names are ... [33]

---

[31] Theodor W. Adorno and Max Horkheimer, *Dialectic of Enlightenment* (trans. John Cumming), (London: Verso, 1979). p. xv.

[32] Theodor W. Adorno, *Minima Moralia: Reflections from Damaged Life* (trans. E. F. N. Jephcott), (London: Verso, 1974). p. 23.

[33] *Calendar of the Carew Manuscripts Preserved in the Archiepiscopal Library at Lambeth*, eds. J.S. Brewer and William Bullen (London: Longmans, 1871), p. 1. (The title-pages of the Rolls Series in which this item appears are misleading:

Despite the collocation of Howth and Fin - not to mention a lengthy digression upon giants, passing reference to King Rory [Roderick] O'Conor known famously to later historians as the "high king with opposition" who made treaty with Henry II in 1175 - and a garbled account of King Mark's difficulties with Tristan, this fascinating book appears not to have caught Joyce's attention. (A copy was certainly in the National Library of Ireland during his student days, and it is cited several times in John Erlington Ball's *Howth and its Owners* [1917].)

The book itself, and Joyce's seeming neglect of it, equally deserve some comment. The original manuscript of *The Book of Howth* forms part of the papers of Sir George Carew, a prominent Elizabethan soldier and statesman in Ireland; it is written in thirteen different hands. Some of it was probably written by a Walter Hussey, and the 7th Lord of Howth (jarl van Hoother, to you) has also been specified as having a hand in its writing. Yet the identification of the scribes leaves untouched the matter of authorship as such, and the matter in the *Book of Howth* is equally impervious to modern classification. Some of it is simply copied from Geraldus Cambrensis; more constitutes redactions (at times highly amusing ones) of semi-legendary material. There is a sly list of "Rebellions that hath been in England" and a poem about the Knights Templar. Near the end there is a splendid digression on Mohammed, followed by a brief section headed "What Ireland is and how much". Finally, according to the editors of the printed text, a hand which does not appear in the body of the book has written at the foot of f. 176 "Finis per me, Ke. Be' He", a transcription which a scholar of our own day declares to be inaccurate though his own version of the sigla will be no less inscrutable.[34]

In provenance, it seems clear that *The Book of Howth* comes from the castle in Howth and that it was composed or compiled over a prolonged period in the sixteenth century. One suggestion is that it was a kind of common-place book in which guests were invited to write down some passage of history, some anecdote or scrap of wisdom - one paragraph recounts the arrival of "a disease called

---

the volume cited here is the fifth in the Carew Calendar, and henceforth is cited as *Carew V*.
The editors comment on the manner and style of *The Book of Howth*:
> In some of the stories it is hard to say whether the writer is giving way to the Irish love of humour and invention, or penning his narrative with one eye to the serious and the other to the ridiculous. Whatever was his purpose, the effect of both is not a little heightened by their juxtaposition so characteristic of Irish history, so unlike that of any other country. (p. xviii)

[34] *Carew V*, p. xii

mases" [measles] and proceeds to list wheat prices. Members of the St. Lawrence family are frequently alluded to, both in the body of the text and in the many marginal summaries and glosses. These include a "Sir Amore Tristerame, now called Saint Larans".[35] Acording to the only twentieth-century commentator to discuss the work at any length:

> In the Book of Howth elaborate descriptions are given of the five battles which Giraldus Cambrensis mentions as fought by John de Courcy in Ulster, and in each case the founder of
> the house of Howth is placed in the forefront, accomplishing wonderful deeds and uttering heroic speeches.[36]

Apart from self-aggrandisement in the manuscript, other details familiar from the *Wake* include Hugh de Lacy.[37] Members of the Howth family are frequently listed in one connection or another, and with them other names from the great families of the Pale, including frequent references to the Nugents of Delvin, and the Nugents as Delvins. For one of the most striking features of *The Book of Howth* is that it takes as its immediate world "Howth Castle and Environs" (*FW* 1.3). Dublin is palpably remote at times; and when the commentary implicitly defines its orbit, this is the Pale, the never entirely fixed area around Dublin in which Anglo-Norman rule was reasonably sovereign. Within it fell most of the counties of Dublin, Meath and Westmeath, together with parts of Kildare and Wicklow and - sometimes - further flung regions. Rarely if ever does anything as western as "the dark mutinous Shannon waves" impinge on the encompassing view from Howth.[38]

As one would expect in a sixteenth-century manuscript written by a dozen hands, spelling and nomenclature vary enormously. There are however stylistic features sufficiently sustained to deserve attention. One is the pithy concentration of the narratives, another the juxtaposition of highly diverse topics and registers of language. The lenghty account of an attempt to convene a parliament illustrates a number of these features as they might have appealed to Joyce, commencing with a marginal caption "A strange dream":

> As the land of Ireland was in good peace under them that were left to keep the land, it befell that a day of Parliament was appointed at a certain place which was taken between Hue de

---

[35] Ibid. pp. 159, 91.
[36] John Erlington Ball, *Howth and its Owners, being the fifth part of A History of County Dublin* (Dublin: At the University Press, 1917), p. 24.
[37] See *FW* 388.33.
[38] James Joyce, *Dubliners* (London: Cape, 1967), p. 255.

Lace, whom the King had given power to keep the land of Ireland with trust, and the King of Mythe. When the Parliament should be, upon the morrow, a knight, whose name was Moriche FitzGerald, now called Robert Griffen by name, thought in his sleep that he saw a much flock of wild swine running upon Hue and Moriche ...

Upon the morrow, they went to the place where as the parliament was set, at a place that men called Rorke's Hill. First, they held their Parliament from far by messengers going between them. Thereafter they by surety of others together ... and they were unweaponed, but the one had swords and the other had their spears, and either of their men was somewhat far from them ...

The traitor O'Rorke had in his mind treason that he had provided and afore made, that he should draw himself by slyght ways from them, and made his excuse for to go piss, and made signs and tokens unto his men that they should come to him in all hasty haste ...

Battle then breaks out; "Greffene and his fellows came running upon their horses stiffly." Linguistic confusion continues, for the account in *The Book of Howth* concludes with a tribute to FitzGerald:

Morich was a man full worshipful and shamefaced visaged, well coloured, comely, little of body, somewhat more than little, much of heart, and of body well fashioned, he had. He wanted nothing of courteous goodness, he was good and loving to all them that loved him ... [39]

In the course of this account Maurice FitzGerald has been renamed Robert Griffen, and has reverted to his old name. Perhaps the post-prandial largesse of Howth Castle is responsible for such confusions of identity, but there is further matter for Joycean exploitation. Another marginal caption deals with a curious coincidence of fate concerning the four leading administrators in Ireland and their heirs. The caption says that "None of the 4 posts of Ireland never had issue mulier", and the entry proper expansively regards this as a wonder apparently pleasing to God and names the four posts. Then the flow of eloquence is abruptly stopped:

This much we have shortly told of John de Coursy; and the other part of his manfulness we leave that to write to others that will it write, saith Camerus, for I will write no more.[40]

---

[39] *Carew V*, pp. 64-66.
[40] Ibid. p. 91.

If, as I believe, Joyce made no use of this extraordinary document in composing his own tale of Howth and Fin, the question is worth asking, Why? Initially, his own absence from Ireland constitutes a partial answer: he was reliant on sources available to him abroad and on sources to which his assistants had reasonable access. The original *Book of Howth* was locked in a London archive, while the printed text was disguised by its position in the sixth volume of the Carew Manuscripts. Of the author of *Howth and its Owners*, however, Joyce knew enough to insert his name at *FW* 55.35 as "elrington bawl". But more thorough-going than thc cffccts of exile were the effects of upbringing and education (including self-education): Joyce's intellectual milieu, even at its most astonishingly receptive, did not often extend into the sixteenth-century history of Ireland. His knowledge of history, and indeed much of his more sophisticated philosophy of it, had distinctly nineteenth-century perimeters. To be sure, he made some use of *The Annals of the Four Masters*, a seventeenth-century Gaelic history. But John O'Donovan's publication of the *Annals* in the middle of the nineteenth century had had a far greater impact on the public mind than the stuffy transcript volumes of the Rolls series. Moreover, the *Annals* were published in several editions, summaries and the like, and the collective name of the scribes had acquired a status of its own. An Elizabethan conquistador's possession of certain Old English memoirs and redactions held little to attract the imagination of any group in late Victorian and Edwardian Ireland. Yet, despite this evident neglect of *The Book of Howth*, Joyce undoubtedly did incorporate into *Finnegans Wake* the St. Lawrence family, their association with the name Tristan or Tristeram, and the focal position of Howth castle gazing into the Pale. Irrespective of a neglected possible source, other affinities were operative.

IV

In conclusion, the question has to be asked, Why should the issue of *Finnegans Wake* and its place in an Irish literary history so persistently avoid texts which Joyce is known to have employed - the original Fenian poems or Moore's Melodies. Beckett's article in *Our Exagmination* insists that 'literary criticism is not book-keeping'[41]: the same ought to be true of literary history - but isn't, for too often Irish literary history has proceeded to chronicle a heritage of debts and borrowings which (curiously enough) is thought to enhance the dignity of all that has gone before. Every writer inserts his work into

---

41 Samuel Beckett "Dante ... Bruno. Vico ... Joyce" in Beckett et al. *Our Exagmination Round his Factification for Incamination of Work in Progress* (London: Faber, 1961) (2nd impr.), p. 4.

a consciously apprehended existing order and, if we are to believe T.S. Eliot, the order is amended in the process. But a more significant order exists at a different level or on a different pitch - one which is not wholly accessible to the individual, or which can be discerned imperfectly if it can be discerned at all. One might refer to this as "the historical unconscious", the material as opposed to the conceptual tradition in which a work exists. Every thriller writer, even the most ignorant, exists within a Virgilian tradition when he commences his story "in medias res". Joyce's use of Irish literary and non-literary texts in *Finnegans Wake* is of course highly varied, and the techniques employed range from mere word-play on a song-title to complex structural analogies such as those involving the Gospels by way of The Book of Kells. However, the notion of literature in its high (and essentially romantic) sense is placed under pressure in the course of Joyce's operations. The annals of Dublin, as summarised in Pettigrew and Oulton's and Thom's Directory, will scarcely be acknowledged as *belles lettres*, though we can be grateful perhaps that Joyce did not get his hands on the baggy and monstrous 19-volume *Calendar of the Ancient Records of Dublin* edited by Lady Gilbert. The Book of Kells may be indisputably a work of art but it is not, in any integral sense, a work of literature. One of the effects which an effort to incorporate *Finnegans Wake* into a literary history must have is to destabilize the serene definition of literature itself.

But an *Irish* literary history not only makes assumptions about the integrity of the literary work, it also presupposes that entity called Ireland. Usually, it presupposes that entity to be a unitary nation. In Ireland, as we have seen, commencement of work on *Finnegans Wake* was closely related to the foundation of such a state to which Joyce declined to return. It is not surprising then to find that the work in progress persistently offers a critique of such imposed presumptions of wholeness and oneness, not only in allusions to the civil war which followed independence but also in the (aptly named) *exploded* view treatment of individual lexical elements. The notion of a national literary history is of course a product of romanticism, and of German romanticism at that. Germany's notorious *disunity* in the romantic era is reflected in the Hegelian insistence that "the whole is the true", a dictum which T.W. Adorno neatly reversed in his *Minima Moralia* to read "the whole is the false".[42] It is sometime remarked that *Finnegans Wake's* circularity is evidence of its perfection of form, or its reconciliation of form and content. It might be better to adopt the spirit of Adorno and recognise the book's insatiable incompleteness, its endless need of itself.

---

[42] Adorno, *Minima Moralia*, p. 50.

That self-resented hermeticism - one thinks of the poetry of Paul Celan also - results from a historical and political situation in which apparent change masks the absence of change and in which the much-deplored "passivity" of the *Wake* maintains a potentiality of praxis. The absence of change, often couched in the language of restoration or the reconciliation of an identity between the actual and the apparent, is of course itself a force felt within history. Epochal change, on the other hand, comes in the shape of a discontinuity, of an arrest apprehended in what has previously continued to be. We measure change by something coming to a halt. The texts I have tried to relate *Finnegans Wake* to stand at certain junctures in Irish cultural history. These are characterised by a discernible plurality of languages and codes, an opposition thought perhaps to be in its nature permanent but in fact highly volatile even in the evidence available to us. The *Book of Howth* comes to us from a period of reluctantly altered loyalties and ironic re-orientations, one in which a host of potent terms and so-called identities are forged. Soon Nugents who were hitherto termed "Old English" become virtual Gaels at the moment of their dispossession from lands they seized from the Gaels. John Erlington Ball, writing of this moment in the life of Christopher, lord of Howth, says:

> A time came when the interests of the Government and those of the chief men of the Pale conflicted, and, notwithstanding the efforts of the Government to attach him to their side, the blind lord was found foremost in defence of his own class.[43]

It is a moment when Elizabethan Realpolitik, administered in Ireland by such poets as Edmund Spenser, Walter Raleigh, and Philip Sidney, turns upon its former mentors. Little more than a century later, Jonathan Swift finds himself at the centre of another political phase of revolutionary change articulating itself as stability and as resistance to monstrous atavism. And less than a century after that, Maria Edgeworth writes a series of fictions sifting the ironies of Union as romantic metaphor, deeply attracted by the consolations of return and reconciliation and the abandonment of difference but - like Swift - she is never finally taken in. *The Book of Howth* is scribally produced within the era of printing but not within a society to which print technology was admitted. *The Absentee* utilises a mass of oral tradition but does so perched on the edge of a technical watershed - between the hand-press and machine-press - which opened out into prospects of a vastly increased readership. With this increase came difficult questions as to what readership, what culture, what country the author might address. To the best of my knowledge, *Finnegans*

---

43 Ball, pp. 73-74.

Wake has only been set in print once; it remains the constant last text of its mode of technical production.

These very cursory placings of a few texts could of course be elaborated to refer to larger economic alterations, the break-down of late-feudal aristocracy, the rise of a mercantile bourgeoisie. However, to conclude, some final emphasis should be laid upon Joyce's position in 1922 when he embarked on *Work in Progress*, though even here one is in the absence of a potential revolution in Irish class relations just as one is in the presence of an actual change in Anglo-Irish state relations. These changes, potential and actual, hinge on the concealed or masked condition of the nineteenth-century middle class in Ireland. Thomas Moore is sometimes called the National Poet. Joyce ensured that he was never elevated as the National Novelist, not even to the extent that Thomas Mann ultimately became the Good German. But the moment he began *Work in Progress* was one of supreme temptation, for there seemed at last a united and independent nation which might serve or be served.

The choice of HCE is a crucial indicator. Hugh Culling Eardley Childers (1827-1896) had been Gladstone's chancellor of the exchequer and home secretary. He gave his name to the House of Commons' Commission (1894-1896) on financial relations between Great Britain and Ireland under the Union. This was the Childers Commission whose evidence of the massive overtaxation of Ireland throughout the nineteenth century so incensed Standish O'Grady. The year 1922 saw *Ulysses* published on the second day of February, and the Irish Free State (Agreement) Act passed on the last day of March. On 14 April, republican forces under Rory O'Connor seized the Four Courts in Dublin; sporadic violence ensued in the Free State, Northern Ireland, and Great Britain. On 22 August Michael Collins, the Free State commander, was ambushed and killed. On 17 November, the Free State government began a series of 77 executions: on 24 November 1922, the government executed by firing squad a leading member of the republican opposition. Known affectionately as "the damned Englishman", he was first cousin once removed to HCE, he was Erskine Childers. (Marcel Proust had died the previous week.) On 8 December, the government executed Rory O'Connor without trial. He was best man in the wedding photograph utilised by Thomas Kinsella in "Nightwalker".

Work in Progress commenced at a time of drastic termination and repression, when the immediate or local agent of such finalities was the presumptive "nation once again". Its author took the bold modernist initiative into decades more typically characterised by the death or defection of earlier pioneers, and he did so stoically conscious of the altering political and cultural conditions in Europe and in Ireland. He began in March 1923, and wrote of Roderick (or Rory) O'Conor:

> the paramount chief polemarch and last pre-electric king of Ireland, who was anything you say yourself between fiftyodd and fiftyeven years of age at the time after the socalled last supper he greatly gave in his umbrageous house of the hundred bottles with the radio beamer tower and its *h*angars, *ch*imbneys and *e*quilines or, at least, he was'nt actually the then last king of all Ireland for the time being for the jolly good reason that he was still such as he was ... (*FW*. 380.11.20) [my italics]

It is a tale of course, a tale already crying out for an ending. But as Patrick Parrinder has judiciously expressed it, "The basic literary mode of the *Wake*, indeed, is historical ..."[44] That is not to say that what Joyce knew was true in some chronicler's sense. But perhaps this consideration of some things he did not know may have convinced us that he knew what he was doing.

W.J.McCormack

---

[44] Patrick Parrinder, *James Joyce* (Cambridge: Cambridge University Press, 1984), p. 217.

Costerus
New Series

Editors: Hans Bertens, C.C. Barfoot, and Theo D'haen

Volume 1
Edited by James L.W. West III. Amsterdam 1974. 194 p.   Hfl. 40,—
Volume 2.
THACKERAY. Edited by Peter L. Shillingsburg. Amsterdam 1974. 359 p.   Hfl. 60,—
Volume 3.
Edited by James L.W. West III. Amsterdam 1975. 184 p.   Hfl. 40,—
Volume 4.
Edited by James L.W. West III. Amsterdam 1975. 179 p.   Hfl. 40,—
Volume 5-6.
GYASCUTUS. Studies in Antebellum Southern Humorous and Sporting Writing. Edited by James L.W. West III. Amsterdam 1978. 234 p.   Hfl. 35,—
Volume 7.
SANFORD PINSKER: The Language of Joseph Conrad. Amsterdam 1978. 87 p.
                                                                        Sold out
Volume 8.
GARLAND CANNON: An Integrated Transformational Grammar of the English Language. Amsterdam 1978. 321 p.   Hfl. 60,—
Volume 9.
GERALD LEVIN: Richardson the Novelist: The Psychological Patterns. Amsterdam 1978. 177 p.   Hfl. 30,—
Volume 10.
WILLIAM F. HUTMACHER: Wynkyn de Worde and Chaucer's Canterbury Tales. A Transcription and Collation of the 1498 Edition with Caxton[2] from the General Prologue Through the Knight's Tale. Amsterdam 1978. 224 p.   Hfl. 40,—
Volume 11.
WILLIAM R. KLINK: S. N. Behrman: The Major Plays. Amsterdam 1978. 272 p.
                                                                        Hfl. 45,—
Volume 12.
VALERIE BONITA GRAY: 'Invisible Man's' Literary Heritage: 'Benito Cereno' and 'Moby Dick'. Amsterdam 1978. 145 p.   Hfl. 30,—
Volume 13.
VINCENT DIMARCO and LESLIE PERELMAN: The Middle English Letter of Alexander to Aristotle. Amsterdam 1978. 194 p.   Hfl. 40,—
Volume 14.
JOHN W. CRAWFORD: Discourse: Essays on English and American Literature. Amsterdam 1978. 200 p.   Hfl. 40,—
Volume 15.
ROBERT F. WILLSON, Jr.: Landmarks of Shakespeare Criticism. Amsterdam 1978. 113 p.   Hfl. 25,—

Volume 16.
A.H. QURESHI: Edinburgh Review and Poetic Truth. Amsterdam 1978. 61 p.Hfl. 15,—
Volume 17.
RAYMOND J.S. GRANT: Cambridge Corpus Christi College 41: The Loricas and the Missal. Amsterdam 1978. 127 p.   Hfl. 30,—
Volume 18.
CARLEE LIPPMAN: Lyrical Positivism. Amsterdam 1978. 195 p.   Hfl. 40,—
Volume 19.
EVELYN A. HOVANEC: Henry James and Germany. Amsterdam 1979. 149 p.
                                                                      Hfl. 30,—
Volume 20.
SANDY COHEN: Norman Mailer's Novels. Amsterdam 1979. 133 p.   Hfl. 25,—
Volume 21.
HANS BERTENS: The Fiction of Paul Bowles. The Soul is the Weariest Part of the Body. Amsterdam 1979. 260 p.   Hfl. 50,—
Volume 22.
RICHARD MANLEY BLAU: The Body Impolitic. A Reading of Four Novels by Herman Melville. Amsterdam 1979. 214 p.   Hfl. 45,—
Volume 23.
FROM CAXTON TO BECKETT: Essays presented by W.H. Toppen on the Occasion of his Seventieth Birthday. Edited by Jacques B.H. Alblas and Richard Todd. With a foreword by A.J. Fry. Amsterdam 1979. 133 p.   Hfl. 30,—
Volume 24.
CAROL JOHNSON: The Disappearance of Literature. Amsterdam 1980. 123 p.
                                                                      Hfl. 25,—
Volume 25.
LINGUISTIC STUDIES offered to Berthe Siertsema. Edited by D.J. van Alkemade, A. Feitsma, W.J. Meys, P. van Reenen en J.J. Spa. Amsterdam 1980. 382 p.   Hfl. 56,—
Volume 26.
FROM COOPER TO PHILIP ROTH. Essays on American Literature. Presented to J.G. Riewald, on the Occasion of his Seventieth Birthday. Edited by J. Bakker and D.R.M. Wilkinson, with a foreword by J. Gerritsen. Amsterdam 1980. 118 p.   Hfl. 25,—
Volume 27.
ALLAN GARDNER SMITH: The Analysis of Motives: Early American Psychology and Fiction. Amsterdam 1980. V,195 p.   Hfl. 40,—
Volume 28.
PATRICK D. MORROW: Tradition, Undercut, and Discovery: Eight Essays on British Literature. Amsterdam 1980. 245 p.   Hfl. 50,—
Volume 29.
THE ROMANTIC AGE OF PROSE. An Anthology. Edited by Alan W. Bellringer and C.B. Jones. Amsterdam 1980. 159 p.   Hfl. 30,—
Volume 30.
P.J. DE VOOGD: Henry Fielding and William Hogarth. The Correspondences of the Arts. Amsterdam 1981. 195 p.   Hfl. 40,—
Volume 31.
GERALD M. BERKOWITZ: Sir John Vanbrugh and the End of Restoration Comedy. Amsterdam 1981. 232 p.   Hfl. 50,—
Volume 32.
C.C. BARFOOT: The Thread of Connection. Aspects of Fate in the Novels of Jane Austen and Others. Amsterdam 1982. 225 p.   Hfl. 45,—

Volume 33.

J.G. RIEWALD AND J. BAKKER: The Critical Reception of American Literature in the Netherlands, 1824-1900. A Documentary Conspectus from Contemporary Periodicals. Amsterdam 1982. 355 p.   Hfl. 70,—

Volume 34.

COLIN PARTRIDGE: The Making of New Cultures: A Literary Perspective. Amsterdam 1982. 131 p.   Hfl. 30,—

Volume 35.

RICHARD S. MOORE: That Cunning Alphabet. Melville's Aesthetics of Nature. Amsterdam 1982. 224 p.   Hfl. 40,—

Volume 36.

JOHN FLETCHER: A Wife for a Moneth. Edited by David Rush Miller. Amsterdam 1983. 286 p.   Hfl. 60,—

Volume 37.

J. BAKKER: Fiction as Survival Strategy. A Comparative Study of the Major Works of Ernest Hemingway and Saul Bellow. Amsterdam 1983. 220 p.   Hfl. 45,—

Volume 38.

HENRY J. DONAGHY: Graham Greene: An Introduction to His Writings. Second edition. Amsterdam 1987. 124 p.   Hfl. 27,50

Volume 39.

WILLIAM COBBETT: A Grammar of the English Language. The 1818 New York first Edition with Passages added in 1819, 1820, and 1823. Edited by Charles C. Nickerson and John W. Osborne. Amsterdam 1983. 185 p.   Hfl. 50,—

Volume 40.

E.M. BEEKMAN: The Verbal Empires of Simon Vestdijk and James Joyce. Amsterdam 1983. III,211 pp.   Hfl. 45,—

Volume 41.

BART WESTERWEEL: Patterns and Patterning. A Study of Four Poems by George Herbert. Amsterdam 1984. 274 pp.   Hfl. 80,—

Volume 42.

COLIN PARTRIDGE: Minor American Fiction 1920-1940. A Survey and an Introduction. Amsterdam 1984. 98 p.   Hfl. 25,—

Volume 43.

THE BEST OF *DQR*. Edited by F.G.A.M. Aarts, J. Bakker, C.C. Barfoot, G. Janssens, M. Buning and W.J. Meys. Amsterdam 1984. 332 pp.   Hfl. 70,—

Volume 44.

JOHN JAMES PEEREBOOM: Fielding Practice. A Study of the Novels of Henry Fielding. Amsterdam 1984. 141 pp.   Hfl. 30,—

Volume 45.

CORPUS LINGUISTICS: Recent Developments in the Use of Computer Corpora in English Language Research. Edited by Jan Aarts and Willem Meijs. Amsterdam 1984. 229 pp.   Hfl. 50,—

Volume 46.

STUDIES IN SEVENTEENTH-CENTURY ENGLISH LITERATURE, HISTORY AND BIBLIOGRAPHY. Festschrift for Professor T.A. Birrell on the Occasion of his Sixtieth Birthday. Edited by G.A.M. Janssens and F.G.A.M. Aarts. Amsterdam 1984. 268 pp.   Hfl. 60,—

Volume 47.

FREDERIC WILL: Shamans in Turtlenecks: Selected Critical Essays 1958-1982. Amsterdam 1984. 299 p.   Hfl. 60,—

Volume 48.
PAGE TO STAGE. *Theatre as Translation*. Edited by Ortrun Zuber-Skerritt. Amsterdam
1984. 200 pp.   Hfl. 45,—
Volume 49.
THE MIRROR OF EVERYMAN'S SALVATION. A Prose Translation of the Original
*Everyman.*Accompanied by *Elckerlijc* and the English *Everyman*. Along with Notes.
Edited by John Conley, Guido de Baere, H.J.C. Schaap, and W.H. Toppen. Amsterdam
1985. 101 pp.   Hfl. 25,—
Volume 50.
SANFORD PINSKER: Conversations with Contemporary American Writers: Saul
Bellow, I.B. Singer, Joyce Carol Oates, David Madden, Barry Beckham, Josephine Miles,
Gerald Stern, Stephen Dunn, Etheridge Knight, Marilynne Robinson, William Stafford.
Amsterdam 1985. 138 pp.   Hfl. 20,—
Volume 51.
ERIC AKKERMAN, PIETER MASEREEUW and WILLEM MEIJS: Designing a
Computerized Lexicon for Linguistic Purposes. Amsterdam 1985. 80 pp.   Hfl. 25,—
Volume 52.
LITERATURE AND LORE OF THE SEA. Edited by Patricia Ann Carlson. Amsterdam
1986. 298 pp.   Paper Hfl. 45,—
                                                                     Bound Hfl. 90,—

Volume 53.
LINGUISTICS AND THE STUDY OF LITERATURE. Edited by Theo D'haen.
Amsterdam 1986. 287 pp.   Paper Hfl. 40,—
                                                                     Bound Hfl. 90,—

Volume 54.
J. BAKKER: Ernest Hemingway in Holland 1925-1981: A Comparative Analysis of the
Contemporary Dutch and American Critical Reception of his Work. Amsterdam 1986. 191
pp.   Hfl. 40,—
Volume 55.
BARBARA FISHER: The House as a Symbol: Joyce Cary and 'The Turkish House'.
Amsterdam 1986. 241 pp.   Hfl. 75,—
Volume 56.
MARIUS BUNING: T.F. Powys: A Modern Allegorist. The companion Novels 'Mr
Weston's Good Wine' and 'Unclay' in the light of modern allegorical theory. Amsterdam
1986. 261 pp.   Hfl. 90,—
Volume 57.
CORPUS LINGUISTICS II. Edited by Jan Aarts & Willem Meijs. Amsterdam 1986. 236
pp.   Hfl. 60,—
Volume 58.
A CENTRE OF EXCELLENCE. Essays Presented to Seymour Betsky. Edited by Robert
Druce. Amsterdam 1987. 216 pp.   Hfl. 55,—
Volume 59.
CORPUS LINGUISTICS AND BEYOND. Proceedings of the Seventh International
Conference on English Language Research on Computerized Corpora. Edited by Willem
Meijs. Amsterdam 1986. 316 pp.   Hfl. 75,—
Volume 60.
CHRISTINE VAN BOHEEMEN-SAAF: Between Sacred and Profane. Narrative design
and the logic of myth from Chaucer to Coover. Amsterdam 1987. 188 pp.   Hfl. 50,—
Volume 61.
BETWEEN DREAM AND NATURE: Essays on Utopia and Dystopia. Edited by
Dominic Baker-Smith and C.C. Barfoot. Amsterdam 1987. 234 pp.   Paper Hfl. 35,—
                                                                     Bound Hfl. 75,—

Volume 62.
EXPLORATIONS IN THE FIELD OF NONSENSE. Edited by Wim Tigges. Amsterdam 1987. 262 pp.   Paper Hfl. 35,—
                                                                                Bound Hfl. 80,—

Volume 63.
ESSAYS ON ENGLISH AND AMERICAN LITERATURE AND A SHEAF OF POEMS will be presented to David R.M. Wilkinson. Edited by Jan Bakker. Amsterdam 1987. 244 pp.   Hfl. 70,—

Volume 64.
ONE HUNDRED YEARS OF ENGLISH STUDIES IN DUTCH UNIVERSITIES. Seventeen papers read at the Centenary Conference Groningen, 15-16 January 1986. Edited by G.H.V. Bunt, E.S. Kooper, J.L. Mackenzie and D.R.M. Wilkinson. Amsterdam 1987. 274 pp.   Hfl. 90,—

Volume 65.
ROLF H. BREMMER JR.: The Fyve Wyttes. A Late Middle English Devotional Treatise. Edited from BL MS Harley 2398 with an Introduction, Commentary and Glossary. Amsterdam 1987. CVI,129 pp.   Hfl. 75,—

Volume 66.
AMERICAN LITERATURE IN BELGIUM. Edited by Gilbert Debusscher. Amsterdam 1987. 274 pp.   Hfl. 60,—

Volume 67.
WIM TIGGES: An Anatomy of Literary Nonsense. Amsterdam 1988. 293 pp. Hfl. 90,—

Volume 68.
GEORGIANA M.M. COLVILLE: Beyond and Beneath the Mantle: On Thomas Pynchon's The Crying of Lot 49. Amsterdam 1988. 119 pp.   Hfl. 38,—

Volume 69.
JOSÉ LANTERS: Missed Understandings. A Study of Stage Adaptations of the Works of James Joyce. Amsterdam 1988. 253 pp.   Hfl. 75,—

Volume 70.
MAUREEN PEECK-O'TOOLE: Aspects of Lyric in the Poetry of Emily Brontë. Amsterdam 1988. 201 pp.   Hfl. 50,—